ART AND MUSIC
A STUDENT'S GUIDE

Paul Munson and Joshua Farris Drake

CROSSWAY

WHEATON, ILLINOIS

Art and Music: A Student's Guide

Copyright © 2014 by Paul Munson and Joshua Farris Drake

Published by Crossway
        1300 Crescent Street
        Wheaton, Illinois 60187

All rights reserved. No part of this publication may be reproduced, stored in a retrieval system, or transmitted in any form by any means, electronic, mechanical, photocopy, recording, or otherwise, without the prior permission of the publisher, except as provided for by USA copyright law.

Cover design: Jon McGrath, Simplicated Studio

First printing 2014

Printed in the United States of America

Unless otherwise indicated, Scripture quotations are from the ESV® Bible (*The Holy Bible, English Standard Version®*), copyright © 2001 by Crossway. 2011 Text Edition. Used by permission. All rights reserved.

Scripture quotations marked KJV are from the *King James Version* of the Bible.

Scripture quotations marked NASB are from *The New American Standard Bible®*. Copyright © The Lockman Foundation 1960, 1962, 1963, 1968, 1971, 1972, 1973, 1975, 1977, 1995. Used by permission.

Scripture quotations marked NIV are taken from *The Holy Bible, New International Version®*, NIV®. Copyright © 1973, 1978, 1984, 2011 by Biblica, Inc.™ Used by permission. All rights reserved worldwide.

Trade paperback ISBN: 978-1-4335-3896-4
ePub ISBN: 978-1-4335-3899-5
PDF ISBN: 978-1-4335-3897-1
Mobipocket ISBN: 978-1-4335-3898-8

Crossway is a publishing ministry of Good News Publishers.

VP		24	23	22	21	20	19	18	17	16	15	14
15	14	13	12	11	10	9	8	7	6	5	4	3	2	1

"The virtues of this book are immediately evident. It asks the right questions, provides the right answers, and illustrates the claims made about art and music with analysis of examples—all within a context of the Christian faith and the Bible."

Leland Ryken, Emeritus Professor of English, Wheaton College

"Drake and Munson know that our minds and imaginations require training to work as intended. They know that failure to cultivate eyes to see and ears to hear prevents us from perceiving the glory of God's creation in great works of art and music. Their book offers courageous instruction for those open to attending to beauty."

Ken Meyers, Director, Mars Hill Audio

"This incredibly thought-provoking book illustrates the relationship between art, music, and spirituality. In our day, it is particularly important to highlight these connections and provide an overall view. I am intrigued by the authors' insights, and others will be as well. I enthusiastically recommend this book."

Manfred Honeck, Music Director, Pittsburgh Symphony Orchestra

ART AND MUSIC

RECLAIMING THE
CHRISTIAN INTELLECTUAL TRADITION

David S. Dockery, series editor

CONSULTING EDITORS

Hunter Baker
Timothy George
Niel Nielson
Philip G. Ryken
Michael J. Wilkins
John D. Woodbridge

OTHER RCIT VOLUMES:

The Great Tradition of Christian Thinking, David S. Dockery and
 Timothy George
The Liberal Arts, Gene C. Fant Jr.
Political Thought, Hunter Baker
Literature, Louis Markos
Ethics and Moral Reasoning, C. Ben Mitchell
Philosophy, David K. Naugle
Christian Worldview, Philip G. Ryken

To
Elizabeth Bedsole
Joseph Blass
Ronald Boud
David Dennis
Dianne Gatwood
Kenneth Hartley (*in memoriam*)
James Richard Joiner
Don W. Martin
C. David McClune
Terry McRoberts
Michael K. Penny
Andy Roby
Georgia Wellborn

with whom we shared those lovely things
we're told to think about—
the sounds with which creation rings—
our friends who find them out.

CONTENTS

SERIES PREFACE

RECLAIMING THE CHRISTIAN INTELLECTUAL TRADITION

The Reclaiming the Christian Intellectual Tradition series is designed to provide an overview of the distinctive way the church has read the Bible, formulated doctrine, provided education, and engaged the culture. The contributors to this series all agree that personal faith and genuine Christian piety are essential for the life of Christ followers and for the church. These contributors also believe that helping others recognize the importance of serious thinking about God, Scripture, and the world needs a renewed emphasis at this time in order that the truth claims of the Christian faith can be passed along from one generation to the next. The study guides in this series will enable us to see afresh how the Christian faith shapes how we live, how we think, how we write books, how we govern society, and how we relate to one another in our churches and social structures. The richness of the Christian intellectual tradition provides guidance for the complex challenges that believers face in this world.

This series is particularly designed for Christian students and others associated with college and university campuses, including faculty, staff, trustees, and other various constituents. The contributors to the series will explore how the Bible has been interpreted in the history of the church, as well as how theology has been formulated. They will ask: How does the Christian faith influence our understanding of culture, literature, philosophy, government, beauty, art, or work? How does the Christian intellectual tradition help us understand truth? How does the Christian intellectual tradition shape our approach to education? We believe that this series is not only timely but that it meets an important need, because the secular culture in which we now find ourselves is, at best, indifferent to the Christian faith, and the Christian world—at least in its more popular forms—tends to be confused about the beliefs, heritage, and tradition associated with the Christian faith.

At the heart of this work is the challenge to prepare a generation of Christians to think Christianly, to engage the academy and the culture, and to serve church and society. We believe that both the breadth and the depth of the Christian intellectual tradition need to be reclaimed, revitalized, renewed, and revived for us to carry forward this work. These study guides will seek to provide a framework to help introduce students to the great tradition of Christian thinking, seeking to highlight its importance for understanding the world, its significance for serving both church and society, and its application for Christian thinking and learning. The series is a starting point for exploring important ideas and issues such as truth, meaning, beauty, and justice.

We trust that the series will help introduce readers to the apostles, church fathers, Reformers, philosophers, theologians, historians, and a wide variety of other significant thinkers. In addition to well-known leaders such as Clement, Origen, Augustine, Thomas Aquinas, Martin Luther, and Jonathan Edwards, readers will be pointed to William Wilberforce, G. K. Chesterton, T. S. Eliot, Dorothy Sayers, C. S. Lewis, Johann Sebastian Bach, Isaac Newton, Johannes Kepler, George Washington Carver, Elizabeth Fox-Genovese, Michael Polanyi, Henry Luke Orombi, and many others. In doing so, we hope to introduce those who throughout history have demonstrated that it is indeed possible to be serious about the life of the mind while simultaneously being deeply committed Christians. These efforts to strengthen serious Christian thinking and scholarship will not be limited to the study of theology, scriptural interpretation, or philosophy, even though these areas provide the framework for understanding the Christian faith for all other areas of exploration. In order for us to reclaim and advance the Christian intellectual tradition, we must have some understanding of the tradition itself. The volumes in this series will seek to explore this tradition and its application for our twenty-first-century world. Each volume contains a glossary, study questions, and a list of resources for further study, which we trust will provide helpful guidance for our readers.

I am deeply grateful to the series editorial committee: Timothy George, John Woodbridge, Michael Wilkins, Niel Nielson, Philip Ryken, and Hunter Baker. Each of these colleagues joins me in thanking our various contributors for their fine work. We all express our appreciation to Justin Taylor, Jill Carter, Allan Fisher, Lane Dennis, and the Crossway team for their enthusiastic support for the project. We offer the project with the hope that students will be helped, faculty and Christian leaders will be encouraged, institutions will be strengthened, churches will be built up, and, ultimately, that God will be glorified.

Soli Deo Gloria
David S. Dockery
Series Editor

+ 1

WHAT DO WE MEAN BY THE WORD *BEAUTY*?

It isn't the likeliest place to find art. The new ballpark is hemmed in on three sides by traffic and on the fourth by a garbage incinerator. The smells of these peripherals are driven out, it's true, by those of flat beer and roller-warmed hot dogs, but this can hardly be said to draw the art-appreciation buffs, who, we're told, prefer wine and cheese. And yet it is there that park designers put a statue of a beloved home-run hitter. No doubt he was amused. The ordinary fellow from an ordinary place, who spoke plainly and lived his life without pretention, now stands 7.5 feet tall in 750 pounds of bronze. A pigeon, unconvinced by the likeness of a batter's high-velocity swing, balances quietly on the cap, leaving an untidy mess. And the boy and his grandfather who stand there on game day know that the statue is *beautiful*—from the pivot of the ankle to the visionary, skyward glance over Sixth Street.

We begin with beauty because it is what makes art, art. When people call something "art," they're saying two things, really: first, that somebody made it (for we don't call accidents "art"), and, second, that its appearance has the potential to reward those who pay attention to it. That is, it can be appreciated for its beauty. If we put a tribal ceremonial mask or a Louis XVI secretary desk in an art museum—indeed, if we use the word *art* to describe a matching outfit and shoes or the perfect baseball swing—it's because we believe that in addition to whatever other functions these things have, they are also beautiful. They provide aesthetic delight.

When the main purpose of a made object is to reward aesthetic contemplation, we call it "high art" or "fine art." We begin with beauty, therefore, because nothing—neither art nor an approach to art—can be evaluated without a sense of what it is for. Although certain philosophers quibble over identifying beauty as the purpose of art, this is only because they fear some people's usage of the word *beauty* may be too constrictive. But ordinary people have always known that the reason we draw and sing is to please viewers with beautiful drawings and hearers with beautiful songs.

Such consensus, however, does not make the idea easy. Beauty has been a central problem in Western thought since the days of Plato and a problem that non-Christians, especially, have difficulty solving. Darwinian materialists may be satisfied that they have found a plausible explanation for the peacock's iridescent plumage. They find it somewhat harder to explain quite why the peahen finds iridescence *especially* sexy. And if her tastes pose some problems, ours pose even more. The materialist cannot explain why a human soul responds as it does to the night sky or to the sound of the sea—or, for that matter, to Rembrandt's *Denial of Peter* in the Rijksmuseum or to Bach's "Gratias agimus tibi" in the Mass in B Minor.

When the artist Makoto Fujimura began studying traditional Japanese nihonga painting as a graduate student in Tokyo during the late 1980s, he was not yet a Christian. One day an assistant professor came into his studio unannounced, looked at the painting Fujimura was working on, said its surface was so beautiful that it was almost terrifying, and walked out. Recalling the incident decades later, Fujimura asks, "Do you know what my response was? I immediately washed the painting down. I couldn't take that. I just didn't have a place for that comment, because, being honest with myself, I felt, if that's true, then I don't have a place in my own heart for beauty that's almost terrifying."[1]

---

[1] Makoto Fujimura, "The Calling of the Artist," talk given at Grove City College, March 18, 2009.

We begin with beauty, frankly, because it drives us to consider the Christian intellectual tradition, which alone gives real answers to the question of how beauty—the source of pleasure—can also terrify. After briefly considering the *classical* and *postmodern* views of beauty that dominate our culture, this first chapter will argue that *Christian* doctrine alone provides a satisfactory explanation of beauty and, thus, a satisfactory explanation of art.

A DESCRIPTIVE DEFINITION

Dictionaries provide descriptive, not prescriptive, definitions. We may or may not like such definitions. We may want to tweak them to conform to what we believe words ought to mean. But there's no doubt that the editors at Merriam-Webster describe rightly when they say that by *beauty*, we mean "the quality or aggregate of qualities in a person or thing that gives pleasure to the senses or pleasurably exalts the mind or spirit."[2] This may or may not tell us what beauty is, but it certainly tells us what people mean by the term. Whenever anyone speaks of "beauty," at the very least he is referring to the capacity of an object to please those who apprehend it.

THE CLASSICAL VIEW OF BEAUTY

In ancient times the equivalent Greek word, *kalos,* worked the same way.[3] Since beauty is considered to be *in the thing perceived,* the classical view concludes that beauty is objective. It is an attribute of the object. Therefore it must be something that can be empirically studied and even measured, as leading Greek thinkers tried to do. The outstanding fifth-century BC sculptor Polycleitos wrote a famous book, now lost, called the *Kanon*, in which he published the numbers of perfect beauty. They were all simple ratios. The

[2] *Merriam-Webster's Collegiate Dictionary*, 11th ed. (Springfield, MA: Merriam-Webster, 2005), s.v. "beauty."

[3] See the colloquial definitions given throughout Plato, *Hippias Major,* and in Aristotle, *Topics,* bk. 6 (146a.21), or the more formal one in Aristotle, *Rhetoric,* bk. 1, chap. 9 (1366a).

analogy to music excited the Pythagoreans, who inferred great significance from the fact that vibrating strings produce harmonious sounds when their lengths are measured in simple proportions. Classical architects planned buildings not with blueprints or elevation drawings but with numerical formulas. All this assumed that beauty is uniform, that all beautiful things are beautiful in the same way. Aristotle taught that "the chief forms of beauty are order and symmetry and definiteness, which the mathematical sciences demonstrate in a special degree."[4] Plato taught not only the uniformity of beauty but also its absolute nature: implicit in the *Republic* and *Phaedrus* and explicit in the *Symposium* is a conflation of the good and the beautiful. The beautiful *is* the good. In such a worldview beauty becomes the very purpose of life, and aesthetics provides the basis for ethics.

This has been the most influential aesthetic position in Western history. Whatever we may think of it, everyone can at least agree that many beautiful things do fit Aristotle's analysis: the symmetries of the human face, for example. Moreover, one can only be thankful for the countless beauties that classicists have dreamed up over the centuries, from the formal clarity of a Botticelli mural to that of Jefferson's Monticello. If we divorce the Parthenon in Athens from its original function to house the goddess, we can treat it as an unparalleled architectural achievement, which in its own way reveals the glory of man's Creator. But make no mistake: not only were the masterpieces of classical antiquity made in the service of idols but also the classical vision itself, at its purest, is an idol. When form is made absolute, when—like the media-bewitched teen starving herself before the mirror—we devote our lives to the pursuit of some created formal standard, the result is not beautiful at all, but wicked and ugly. Hear C. S. Lewis's warning against aestheticism: "These things—the beauty, the memory of our own past—are good images of what we really desire; but if they are

---

[4] Aristotle, *Metaphysics*, bk. 13 (1078b).

mistaken for the thing itself, they turn into dumb idols, breaking the hearts of their worshippers."[5]

But this is not the only critique of classicism. The classical view of beauty may be dominant in the Western tradition, with neoclassical movements peculiar to every era, but every era also produced its own alternative to the classical vision. And it's easy to see why. Every reader, surely, can think of things he knows to be beautiful, even though they are not ordered or not symmetrical or not definite: a thunderstorm, say, or a clear, blue sky. How are we to explain the beauty of these? Nineteenth-century romantics, to cite just one alternative, saw the sublime—that which fills us with awe—as a higher aesthetic category than those of classicism. They preferred the Swiss Alps to English formal gardens. Yet neither romanticism nor any other reaction against classicism has provided a viable explanation for *all* human experiences of beauty. Can a scheme that accounts for our reaction to Victoria Falls and the Pleiades also account for the aesthetic value of something as comfortable and domestic as a lullaby or a quilt?

THE POSTMODERN VIEW OF BEAUTY

Who, then, can tell what beauty is? We've only mentioned the classical position and, in passing, the romantic critique of it, but of course every culture and every worldview has its own aesthetic values. How could any one explanation account for all instances of beauty? In the pluralistic 1980s and 90s the problems of beauty came to seem insurmountable. Indeed, the descriptive definition seems to contradict itself. Read it again. *Beauty* is "the quality or aggregate of qualities in a person or thing that gives pleasure to the senses or pleasurably exalts the mind or spirit." The first half locates beauty in the thing perceived, whereas the second half links it to pleasure—which is something that takes place *inside the perceiver,* not in the thing perceived. So which is it? Is beauty a quality

---
[5] C. S. Lewis, *The Weight of Glory* (New York: Touchstone, 1996), 29.

of the perceived object or a quality of the perceiving subject? It can't be both. Something cannot be both objective and subjective, except perhaps in Hinduism. Since what pleases me may not be what pleases you, postmoderns have roundly rejected the opening phrase of the definition. To the postmodern, beauty is in fact a quality of the subject—a quality of the one looking, not of the thing being seen. It's the sensation I have whenever I perceive something I like.[6] It is just a matter of taste, which cannot be accounted for, except by sociologists who study how we are culturally conditioned to consider some things beautiful and not other things. Beauty is in the eye of the beholder.

Let's think about that adage for a minute. It's of fairly recent origin (late nineteenth century). But we have so imbibed postmodern relativism that most people think of this adage not as a matter of worldview but as a truism. The best way to learn its meaning is to consider *when* we say it: invariably in the midst of a dispute over the aesthetic worth of something, and it has the effect of ending the dispute. For if beauty exists in the beholder—in you and me, and not in the thing under dispute—then why are we disputing? Nobody argues about subjective phenomena. We don't argue about whether you are hungry or whether I'm afraid.

The adage performs a metaphysical sleight of hand. Throughout human history cultures have felt the need for some category corresponding to this English word *beauty*. It provides the basis for all critical thinking about form and preference. How do we know that some preferences are better than others? Well, we assess the beauty of the thing preferred. Drug addicts prefer intoxication. Intoxication is manifestly not beautiful. Therefore we know something is wrong with their preference. Without a

---

[6] For an early formulation of this position see Curt Ducasse, "The Subjectivity of Aesthetic Value" (1929), in *Introductory Readings in Aesthetics*, ed. John Hospers (New York: Free Press, 1969). For a statement of this position by a practicing artist, see Louise Bourgeois, "Sunday Afternoons: A Conversation and a Remark on Beauty," in *Uncontrollable Beauty: Toward a New Aesthetics,* ed. Bill Beckley (New York: Allworth, 2002), 331.

concept of beauty, we could still call any *action* motivated by their preference immoral (provided we still have a concept of the good), but we couldn't criticize the preference itself. In short, the idea of beauty is what allows us to call an appetite for bad things wrongheaded. But the adage (which almost everybody assumes to be true) would remind us that beauty and preference are the same thing. When we act as if beauty were an objective standard by which we can judge preferences, we are—it seems—just playing a mental game that arbitrarily privileges our preferences over other people's preferences, for any argument about the healthiness of certain preferences is circular. End of discussion. Now we can all get along.

To postmoderns, beauty is therefore no longer a matter for serious reflection and study. For the first time in history, many respectable artists cannot care less whether their work is beautiful. Yet, in Christian circles, postmoderns are frequently said to care more about aesthetics than they do about morality and the truth. When people say this, what they mean is that postmoderns are more persuaded by how attracted they are to a proposition than by how well it conforms to God's law or to the principles of logic. There are two problems with this way of speaking. First, it describes something not new to postmodernism; we human beings have always believed what we want to believe even in the face of a contrary reality (Romans 1). The second problem with this way of speaking is that it adopts the postmodern usage of these terms. If you criticize postmoderns for caring more about beauty than about goodness or truth, when you *mean* that they care more about their own preferences than they do about goodness or truth, your thinking has been colored by the postmodern take on beauty. You've made it a synonym for preference. In fact no movement in history has been more hostile to beauty than postmodernism. One of the most celebrated anthologies of postmodern cultural thought from the 1980s was entitled *The Anti-Aesthetic,* in recognition that now politics had displaced beauty as the essence of art.[7] It turns out that what is new in postmodernism is not a prioritizing of the beautiful over the good and the true but rather a revolt against authority of any kind—a revolt as much against the beautiful as against the good and the true. A revolt against reality itself.

A corollary of this is that we are also mistaken when we talk about how visually oriented the current generation is. One frequently hears that postmoderns are more disposed to understand through images than through words and propositions. And yet this has not been borne out by our experience as teachers of art history and appreciation; we find many students to be insecure in their ability to see some of the most basic things in pictures. However prominent visual media are in our society, they do surprisingly little to hone our powers of sight. Quite the contrary. It turns out that postmoderns do not neglect words for the sake of images. Rather, they neglect all communicative forms, both verbal and visual. If you want to attract a postmodern audience, sure, use pictures. Use words. Just see to it that the pictures and words don't say very much. For we have come to distrust meaning itself. We have come to associate authenticity with an incommunicative formlessness. The less a form says, the more sincere it is.

Now, in these matters, is the church different from the world? American evangelicals in the twentieth century were pretty faithful in asserting the importance of truth and goodness. Most grew up knowing that it was not up to them to define what these things were. Truth and goodness were part of an external reality to which one had to submit, if one wasn't going to go about constantly bruising one's shins in a self-inflicted psychosis. So what about beauty? Early on, we Christians bought into postmodernity's aesthetic relativism hook, line, and sinker. Some still fight for goodness and truth; we know that the goodness of God's will and the

---

[7] Hal Foster, ed., *The Anti-Aesthetic: Essays on Postmodern Culture* (Port Townsend, WA: Bay Press, 1983).

truth of his Word are absolute, but the forms they take are said to be culturally determined and morally neutral.[8] Wasn't it the Pharisees who cared about form? As long as we get the substance of the gospel right, it does not matter how we proclaim it, or so we think. But we're inconsistent. For all our aesthetic relativism, we fight over forms today as much as ever. It's just that now we have a guilty conscience about it, because deep inside we have come to think that forms have little to do with the "big" issues.

THE CHRISTIAN VIEW OF BEAUTY

It has not always been this way. In Mark 14:3–8, Jesus assumed that beauty is more than preference but something objective and important—so much so that it ought to play a role in the disciples' ethical decision making:

> And while he was at Bethany in the house of Simon the leper, as he was reclining at table, a woman came with an alabaster flask of ointment of pure nard, very costly, and she broke the flask and poured it over his head. There were some who said to themselves indignantly, "Why was the ointment wasted like that? For this ointment could have been sold for more than three hundred denarii and given to the poor." And they scolded her. But Jesus said, "Leave her alone. Why do you trouble her? She has done a beautiful thing to me. For you always have the poor with you, and whenever you want, you can do good for them. But you will not always have me. She has done what she could; she has anointed my body beforehand for burial."

The word *kalos*, translated in verse 6 as "beautiful" by the ESV and NIV, literally means that. Elsewhere, New Testament authors frequently employ the word in its secondary or figurative sense of "good," which is how the KJV and NASB translate it here. Even then the focus is on goodness of use or goodness of appearance,

---

[8] See, e.g., Harold M. Best, *Music through the Eyes of Faith* (San Francisco: HarperSanFrancisco, 1993), 42–47.

the word for intrinsic goodness being *agathos*. But we need not speculate here, for Jesus explained himself. He did not commend the woman merely for the goodness of her deed. It wasn't just that she worshiped him or that she worshiped him sincerely. Jesus commended her for the way (or form) in which she worshiped him. "She has anointed my body beforehand for burial." That is, she worshiped him in a way that acknowledged what everyone else still seemed to be in denial about: that the Son of Man came to give his life, and the hour was now at hand. Does it seem strange that the Lord would commend someone specifically for the *beauty* of her deed?

It did not seem strange to Christians in ages gone by. Until recently, it was taken for granted that form matters to God. Psalm 27:4 calls God himself beautiful. His glory is one of the most important themes in the Bible, and any Bible dictionary will tell you that God's glory—*kabod* in the Old Testament and *doxa* in the New—is his perfections put on display. (Is God really beautiful? Don't be shocked by the question. Many thoughtful evangelicals today, when pressed, will deny that God is beautiful in order to be consistent in their aesthetic relativism. When the Bible speaks this way, they reason, it's just using a figure of speech to describe the pleasure Christians happen to experience in him. Theirs is a radically new way to think about the attributes of God.)

The Bible also asserts that God's creation is beautiful. "He has made everything beautiful in its time" (Eccles. 3:11). It is only our sin that brought ugliness into the world and blinds us to the beauty all around. Why did God make all things beautiful? Psalms 8 and 19, Acts 14, and Romans 1 teach us that he did so to reflect his own beauty. And if God is beautiful, and if his creation is beautiful, then there is an objective measure for beauty, and we can think critically about it.

Here we have what can be called the historic Christian view of beauty. We do not hesitate to call it *the* Christian view because it's obviously that of all our best thinkers, from Augustine to Aquinas to Calvin to Edwards.[9] If we may be so bold as to put the Christian definition of beauty in our own words, it is *the forms through which we recognize the nature and ways of God*. Whereas the classical view equates beauty with goodness and truth, and the postmodern view separates beauty from goodness and truth, the Christian view asserts that they always go together, even as it draws an important distinction between them. Thus the common word *beauty* is very closely related to the theological idea of *revelation*, both general and special. Just as revelation communicates to man the truth concerning God and his will, so beauty is the form of that communication. For example, when we study the heavens and discover their beauty, essentially what has happened is that we have perceived in their form a kind of speech that declares the glory of God. Similarly, the Christian doctrine of beauty is implicit in the very first chapter of Genesis. When God made the world, he "saw" that it was good. Creation had a form that made goodness visible.

BACK TO THE DESCRIPTIVE DEFINITION

In contrast to the postmodern, then, the Christian sees no contradiction at all in the descriptive definition of "beauty," because he believes humans were made to take pleasure in certain things, namely, in God's goodness. You may think something is pleasant, and I may think something else is pleasant, but one or both of us may not know what true pleasure is. In fact, we may be drawn to that which will make us miserable. It's precisely because we are so prone to deceive ourselves about pleasure that we need the concept of beauty. It enables us to think critically about pleasure, which, by the way, is why postmoderns hate beauty so much and want to

[9] Augustine, Letter 166 (to Jerome, on the origin of the soul), chap. 5; and *De Vera Religione* 32. Thomas Aquinas, *Commentary on the Divine Names* 4.5; and *Summa Theologica* 1.39.8 reply. John Calvin, *Institutes of the Christian Religion*, trans. Ford Lewis Battles (Philadelphia: Westminster, 1960), 1.5.1–19 and 3.10.1–6. Jonathan Edwards, *A Treatise concerning Religious Affections*, pt. 3, sec. 4; and *A Dissertation Concerning the Nature of True Virtue,* chap. 3.

conflate it with preference. They don't want to have to think critically about pleasure. They don't want any reminders that their joys aren't solid, that their treasures won't last.

POSTMODERN OBJECTIONS TO
THE CHRISTIAN VIEW

Furthermore, postmoderns see critical thought as a threat to human diversity. If beauty is objective, they wonder, what ought we to make of differing preferences? If Tim likes something and Sally doesn't, is one of them wrong? If beauty is objective, would this not produce a cookie-cutter approach, in which everybody is supposed to like the same things? Did not God make us uniquely in his image, so we can each glorify him in our own way? Yes, he did. Many who still claim truth to be objective do not wrestle with similar questions regarding truth; after all, what could be more diverse or more objective than the truths "two plus two is four" and "strawberries are sweet"? These fears are based on a fallacious (or should we say classical?) assumption that objectivity means uniformity.

In the Christian view, beauty is endlessly diverse because it manifests an infinite glory. Moreover, everybody's approach to this endless diversity is different, because God endows each with a unique constitution and background. It's only to be expected—and, indeed, it's good—that we have different preferences. The reason individuals and cultures differ in their notions of beauty is not that its essence is up for grabs but that no finite (not to mention fallen) mind can comprehend it in its fullness. The historic Christian understanding of beauty acknowledges not just that beauty is objective but that it is *transcendentally* objective. It is an object bigger than we—infinitely bigger than we—so we all see different aspects of it. And, as we do so, more of God's glory is beheld than if we all saw the same things. As it turns out, the Christian doctrine of beauty provides the only true basis for diversity.

Many today embrace aesthetic relativism as a way to foster tolerance and respect, but what relativism really fosters is indifference. If no form is better than any other, then the beauties I already know suffice, and I don't need to learn from anyone else. If I am an aesthetic relativist—consistent in my relativism—and you come to me this afternoon and say, "Oh, you've got to come outside and see the sky—it's beautiful," my response will be, "Who do you think you are, to think you have seen something that I would be better off for seeing, too?" The Christian view, by contrast, humbles us. It teaches us that we need one another. If we are going to see as much of God's glory as possible, we have to learn to see through others' eyes.

Consider the following illustration. Five-year-old Billy carefully draws a picture for his mother. When he brings it to her, what will she say? "Oh, Billy, it's beautiful." But if the curator of an art museum walks by, he will take no notice of Billy's drawing. Since you and I would condone both of these responses, the postmodern says, "Aha, gotcha. If the drawing is beautiful to Billy's mom and ugly to the curator, its beauty depends on who's perceiving it." But let's consider what it would look like to apply consistently each of the main doctrines of beauty in this situation. To the classicist, either the mother is being dishonest with Billy or she is deluding herself. The postmodern, meanwhile, will commend both the mother and the curator for being true to themselves and for finding beauty and ugliness wherever they are so inclined. However, on the same grounds, the postmodern would also have to commend the mother if she had said, "Billy, this is the ugliest thing I've ever seen." Likewise the postmodern would have to commend the curator if he had chosen to discard a Rembrandt to make room for the "Billy." Only the Christian view accords with what we know to be right. The mother is right to see how the form of Billy's drawing reveals objectively good things: his love for her, his imagination, and the development of his fine motor skills. If any of us made the effort to look—really look—at Billy's drawing, we would see these things, too. The mother does not project beauty onto the drawing. It's there. But the curator has a different purpose for drawings. His job is to find and to display those images that will most reward aesthetic contemplation, a purpose for which Billy's drawing is ill-suited. So both are right, without making the beauty and the ugliness which they saw subjective.

Remember, the beauty of any object is its capacity to proclaim truth and to realize goodness. The ugliness of any object is the sum of all the ways in which it obscures truth and impedes goodness, which means that everything in this cursed world is both beautiful and ugly. Some things will be mostly beautiful, and some will be mostly ugly, but everything will be a mix, because there are multiple purposes—both good purposes and evil purposes—to which any object can be put. This means, for example, that something ugly can be depicted beautifully—say, in a movie about the Holocaust—if the ugliness and the evil are depicted accurately. If we learn from it anew how vile sin is, how real judgment is, and how near grace is, then a depiction of ugliness can be very beautiful indeed. And only the Christian view of beauty can account for this.

CONCLUSION

So Christian doctrine provides the only satisfactory explanation of beauty. It tells us what beauty is and why we respond emotionally to beauty, even as it prevents us from making an idol of beauty. The Christian view provides the only true basis for aesthetic diversity and humility. It provides the only satisfactory explanation of ugliness. And it also provides a way to resolve aesthetic disputes. Here, the first step is to agree on what the disputed object is *for*. When we argue over form, we sometimes talk past each other, assuming our disagreement to be aesthetic in nature when often it's really ethical. Once we have agreed on a common purpose, however, it should be a fairly straightforward—even scientific—process to determine what form can most effectively realize that purpose. If both parties do in fact share a common purpose but cannot resolve their conflict, it can only be that one or both lack aesthetic discernment. We are not born aesthetically wise. It is something we must learn through diligent study and repentance.

The postmodern, however, sees no need for repentance, for if beauty is what I make of it rather than an external reality, then beauty demands nothing of me. The end of aesthetic relativism is aesthetic immaturity. Mind you, this describes more than nonbelievers. It also describes Bible-believing Christians who have adopted the world's aesthetic relativism, which is in fact aesthetic rebellion. Compared to our forebears in the faith we are aesthetically immature. Consider clothing, for example. Historically Christians have understood that clothing speaks (just as the heavens do) and that our main consideration in choosing clothes should be the well-being of those who have to look at us. Today, however, we regularly show up in public dressed as if we're going to garden or change the oil in our car. Male students in our classrooms intentionally comb their hair to make it look like they didn't comb it. Their studied carelessness sends an unintended message. It says: "I don't want you to think that I love you enough to try to bless you with a pleasant appearance." We can observe the same pattern in all the great social endeavors of commerce, governance, education, worship, and family life.

But don't stop there. It's not just human communication that falters. We grow insensitive to the forms through which God himself communicates. The Catholic theologian Hans Urs von Balthasar described the tragedy most clearly:

> Our situation today shows that beauty demands for itself at least as much courage and decision as do truth and goodness, and she will not allow herself to be separated and banned from her two sisters without taking them along with herself in an act of mysterious vengeance. . . . In a world without beauty—even if

people cannot dispense with the word and constantly have it on the tip of their tongues in order to abuse it—in a world which is perhaps not wholly without beauty, but which can no longer see it or reckon with it: in such a world the good also loses its attractiveness, the self-evidence of why it must be carried out. Man stands before the good and asks himself why it must be done and not rather its alternative, evil. For this, too, is a possibility, and even the more exciting one: Why not investigate Satan's depths? In a world that no longer has enough confidence in itself to affirm the beautiful, the proofs of truth have lost their cogency. In other words, syllogisms may still dutifully clatter away like rotary presses or computers which infallibly spew out an exact number of answers by the minute. But the logic of these answers is itself a mechanism which no longer captivates anyone. The very conclusions are no longer conclusive.[10]

Aesthetic relativism is an attack on revelation resulting in moral and epistemological relativism.

Where does it come from? Sins like sloth, lust, and pride may play a part, but most fundamentally our attraction to aesthetic relativism suggests an aversion to God's glory. Could it be that we hate beauty because we hate God? That we hate real pleasure?[11] This is where the Christian view of beauty proves to be not just philosophically satisfying but evangelistically necessary, for the gospel applies to all of life, including aesthetics. In 2 Corinthians 3, Paul defends the high view he takes of his ministry by comparing it to the ministry of Moses. In verse 7 he begins specifically to compare the way the glory of God was perceived in the old covenant with the way it is perceived in the new. Picking up in verse 12:

> Since we have such a hope, we are very bold, not like Moses, who
> would put a veil over his face so that the Israelites might not gaze

---

[10] Hans Urs von Balthasar, *The Glory of the Lord*, vol. 1 (San Francisco: Ignatius, 1982), 18–19.
[11] The English philosopher Roger Scruton asks this question with startling honesty but no Christian answers in "The Flight from Beauty," the eighth chapter of his book *Beauty* (Oxford, UK: Oxford University Press, 2009).

at the outcome of what was being brought to an end.[12] But their minds were hardened. For to this day, when they read the old covenant, that same veil remains unlifted, because only through Christ is it taken away. Yes, to this day whenever Moses is read a veil lies over their hearts. But when one turns to the Lord, the veil is removed. Now the Lord is the Spirit, and where the Spirit of the Lord is, there is freedom. And we all, with unveiled face, beholding the glory of the Lord, are being transformed into the same image from one degree of glory to another. For this comes from the Lord who is the Spirit.

Paul refers to Exodus 34. What happened to those who, in the old covenant, encountered the glory of God? They became conscious of their doom and their need for a mediator. Without Christ, they needed a veil to obstruct their view of the glory because they *could not* look at its outcome: death for sinners (v. 7). Every generation has its own favorite way of avoiding glory; the Pharisees had their legalism, moderns had their materialism, and postmoderns have their relativism. But it's a temporary fix. Only in Christ is the moth not crushed. He took upon himself the outcome of sin's encounter with glory so that we can behold it without being damned. No longer needing a veil, we are free to enjoy him. "For God, who said, 'Let light shine out of darkness,' has shone in our hearts to give the light of the knowledge of the glory of God in the face of Jesus Christ" (2 Cor. 4:6).

---

[12] The NIV's paraphrase of v. 13 misleads: "We are not like Moses, who would put a veil over his face to keep the Israelites from gazing at it while the radiance was fading away." This reading in English implies that what Moses was covering up was the *fading away* rather than the *glory*. Did Moses try to conceal the fact that the glory was impermanent? This implication is made explicit in the *NIV Study Bible* ([Grand Rapids, MI: Zondervan, 2002] note for 3:13). Yet this reading is not required by the Greek, finds no support in pre-modern commentaries, and would be irrelevant to Paul's argument at this point. Ex. 34:30 and 2 Cor. 3:7 indicate that Moses was covering the glory, because the outcome (*telos*) of that glory was death. The fact that the glory was coming to an end (in contrast to the permanence of glory of God in the face of Jesus Christ) is just another point of comparison between Moses's and Paul's ministries.

2

WHY SHOULD WE ENJOY ART AND MUSIC?

Ecclesiastes 2:1–11 reads like a dismissal of culture and, in particular, of leisure:

> I said in my heart, "Come now, I will test you with pleasure; enjoy yourself." But behold, this also was vanity. I said of laughter, "It is mad," and of pleasure, "What use is it?" I searched with my heart how to cheer my body with wine—my heart still guiding me with wisdom—and how to lay hold on folly, till I might see what was good for the children of man to do under heaven during the few days of their life. I made great works. I built houses and planted vineyards for myself. I made myself gardens and parks, and planted in them all kinds of fruit trees. I made myself pools from which to water the forest of growing trees. I bought male and female slaves, and had slaves who were born in my house. I had also great possessions of herds and flocks, more than any who had been before me in Jerusalem. I also gathered for myself silver and gold and the treasure of kings and provinces. I got singers, both men and women, and many concubines, the delight of the sons of man. So I became great and surpassed all who were before me in Jerusalem. Also my wisdom remained with me. And whatever my eyes desired I did not keep from them. I kept my heart from no pleasure, for my heart found pleasure in all my toil, and this was my reward for all my toil. Then I considered all that my hands had done and the toil I had expended in doing it, and behold, all was vanity and a striving after wind, and there was nothing to be gained under the sun.

Laughter, wine, houses, horticulture, animal husbandry, wealth, and music all proved useless to the Preacher. They were for him a kind of madness: "a striving after wind." But how can this be, given what the Scriptures say elsewhere about these things?

- In Luke 6:21 Jesus uses laughter to describe those who enjoy the favor of God. "Blessed are you who weep now, for you shall laugh."
- John 2 describes how Jesus "manifested his glory" by miraculously providing good wine at a wedding celebration.
- In Jeremiah 29:5 God tells the exiles in Babylon to "build houses and live in them; plant gardens and eat their produce."
- Elsewhere God promises flourishing herds and flocks to the remnant of his people who repent and dwell in Zion. For example, in Isaiah 30:23 he says, "In that day your livestock will graze in large pastures."
- Silver and gold, too, can be a blessing. In Genesis 24:35 Abraham's servant says, "The LORD has greatly blessed my master, and he has become great. He has given him flocks and herds, silver and gold, male servants and female servants, camels and donkeys."
- As for singing, well, all God's people are singers by definition. About a hundred times in Scripture, we are urged to make music. For example, back in Isaiah 30 the remnant is told, "You shall have a song as in the night when a holy feast is kept" (v. 29).

Interpreting Scripture with Scripture, we see that the most straightforward reading of Ecclesiastes 2 cannot be the correct one. The kinds of culture and leisure in question are not necessarily vain but can be a major component of the abundant life Christ intends for us to have. The passage from Ecclesiastes 2 does give us a clue to its proper interpretation even without the help of the other Scriptures, but we must look closely at what is actually being said there.

Verse 1, taken with verse 11, tells us that to "enjoy yourself" is vanity. What the ESV translates as "enjoy yourself," the King James Version translates as "enjoy pleasure." So which is it? As it turns out, both are right. The two Hebrew words, *ra'ah towb*, literally mean "to see or consider a good or pleasant thing," but in the context of the Preacher's discourse, the translators of the ESV and KJV rightly notice that something more than that is being said. The two translations (which date from 2001 and 1611) describe, respectively, the postmodern and classical errors about beauty, both of which are then condemned as vanity.

Taking the ESV's translation, we know that "enjoy yourself" is exactly what the postmodern aims at. He does not enjoy laughter, wine, or houses. He enjoys himself. If beauty is subjective, then only the subject is left as an object of enjoyment. And of course this is vanity. Taking the KJV's translation, we describe exactly what the ancient Greeks did. They "enjoy[ed] pleasure." Seeing beauty as something in the object itself, and setting their eyes on it alone, they "exchanged the glory of the immortal God for images resembling mortal man and birds and animals and creeping things" (Rom. 1:23). Pleasure is merely a by-product of our enjoyment of God. To pursue it, rather than God, is, as Lewis put it, to have our hearts broken. The Christian doctrine of leisure avoids both of the pitfalls expressed alternatively in these translations. It teaches us that all things were made for God's glory, and we find joy in them only insofar as we enjoy God through them. Hence the Preacher concludes in verses 24–25: "There is nothing better for a person than that he should eat and drink and find enjoyment in his toil. This also, I saw, is from the hand of God, for apart from him who can eat or who can have enjoyment?"

Elsewhere the Bible gives us models of such godly leisure. Adam was put in a garden, which implies both work and contemplative leisure. David, the man after God's heart, played the lyre "day by day" (1 Sam. 18:10). Jesus celebrated weddings. He "came eating and drinking" (Matt. 11:19). Paul, in an aside, affirms that wealthy Christians may enjoy God's material gifts: "As for the rich in this present age, charge them not to be haughty, nor to set their hopes on the uncertainty of riches, but on God, who richly provides us with everything to enjoy" (1 Tim. 6:17; see also 4:3–4). What

1 Timothy 6 teaches us is that pleasure in its proper place is a good thing. More importantly, it teaches wherein pleasure is found: neither in ourselves nor, ultimately, in the thing that mediates pleasure, but in the Lord. Perhaps here is the basis for distinguishing between idleness (Prov. 31:27; 2 Thess. 3:6–7) and what we might call "recreation" (Gen. 24:63; Ps. 8:3). Idleness is enjoying oneself or the pleasures themselves. Recreation is enjoyment of God, which is part of our chief end.

We enjoy God by pondering his ways (Ps. 77:12). We study his Word, which theologians call "special revelation," and we study his works of creation and providence, which theologians call "general revelation." God intends the two kinds of revelation to go together, and each is incomplete without the other. Without the good news of the gospel found in the Bible, the wonders of nature and culture only serve to intensify our alienation from God; we cannot bear such clear examples of the goodness, wisdom, and power of the one we hate. To quote Calvin, "People, immersed in their own errors, are struck blind in such a dazzling theater."[1] But when the Lord makes known his salvation, all the earth makes a joyful noise as in Psalm 98 (on which Isaac Watts's hymn "Joy to the World" is based). "Let the sea roar, and all that fills it. . . . Let the rivers clap their hands; let the hills sing for joy together before the LORD, for he comes to judge the earth."

Conversely, without the wonders of nature and culture, the Bible is unintelligible. What urgency would the gospel have if we had no existential knowledge of God or any idea of our filth and alienation from him? Why would we care about God's redemptive purposes? Indeed, sensitivity to general revelation is necessary to appreciate any page of Scripture. Psalm 1 says that the blessed man is like a tree. But what could that possibly mean to someone who is ignorant of, or indifferent to, trees? It seems likely that when God

---

[1] John Calvin, *Institutes of the Christian Religion*, trans. Ford Lewis Battles (Philadelphia: Westminster, 1960), 1.5.8.

made trees on the third day of creation, part of his purpose was to design a picture of what the blessed man is like. In the book of Job, the Lord answers his great questions—our questions—with an appeal to general revelation (Job 38–41). Jesus teaches us about anxiety by telling us to "consider the lilies" (Matt. 6:28).

There can be little doubt that *the leisurely contemplation of general revelation is an essential part of the Christian life* and that our capacity for joy depends, in part, on our being good stewards of leisure. A happy person's leisure will include the direct study of creation (in woodland walks, for example, or in a butterfly collection or in a fun math problem) and of providence (in history), but such a happy person will also learn from other people how to appreciate revelation. The literary and scientific achievements of human culture can, despite their fallibility, aid us in contemplating the glory of God. So, too, can the arts. What follows, then, are four reasons, based on the Christian doctrine of general revelation, why we should enjoy art and music.

REASON 1: ARTISTS AND MUSICIANS EXPOUND GENERAL REVELATION IN MUCH THE SAME WAY THAT PREACHERS EXPOUND SPECIAL REVELATION

A comparison to the preaching of God's Word works very well. Though God's Word is open to all believers, not every believer is equally gifted in or trained especially for the reading and understanding of it. Likewise, though the invisible attributes of God are clearly seen in the things that are made (Rom. 1:20)—even by nonbelievers, let alone believers—some people are especially gifted at observing particular things about general revelation. When the things they observe are mathematical, we call those people "mathematicians." When the things are marine, we call those people "mariners." But when those things relate to patterns of sound, we call those people "musicians." A composer takes pitches and rhythms and organizes them according to principles of design apparent in nature. Trunk is to twig as symphony is to melody. A great piece of music, through its interrelationship of parts, is a little world of its own, echoing imperfectly the world after which it was patterned—which world echoes the Creator. How music does this is the work of chapter 5 of this book. Likewise, the visual artist, whose work is described in chapter 4, has peculiar gifts that make him able to see better than we. He is also able, through the disciplines of his art, to report back to us what he sees in a way that will make our seeing more clear. He draws our attention to significant features of things, sometimes by means of exaggeration or even abstraction, to show us the nature of those things. He uses shapes and colors, not words, to do this. Just as preachers use words to talk about God's Word, so artists and composers make "works" to talk about God's works.

Now, we should come clean at the outset and say that just as third-born sons of the nineteenth-century English gentry were able to make a living as preachers, and the farmers and fishermen they preached to were willing to put up with their inanity, so too the charlatan artist of twenty-first-century London will be able to make a living at his "craft," thanks to the fashionable rich who thoughtlessly praise his work. Nor do we pretend that even competent and expressive nonbelieving artists are able to admit that it is God's glory about which they report in their art; they suppress this knowledge (Rom. 1:21). Yet just because something can be done badly or from the wrong motivation does not mean that it is always done badly or that bad motivation necessarily mars the outcome. The Roman emperor may hand out bread from a fear of uprising or from a love for the people; the bread will taste the same either way.

Many are concerned that in the face of possible charlatanry in art and music, they might not be competent to tell the difference between a work of art that reports a great deal about the basic designs of nature and a work that reports almost nothing. Scripture comes to our aid in this and all epistemological crises. Psalm 19, for instance, tells us that the heavens *declare* the glory of the Lord.

They don't merely hint at it, leaving us without model for good art and music. In his exhortation to the Philippians, Paul tells them to think on whatever things are lovely (4:8). This assumes that they have some idea of what is lovely and what is not. The problem is not that we cannot tell the difference between the sham art and the real, but that, having distinguished the two, we nevertheless choose the sham art. Most people have the ability to know the difference between a good sermon and a bad one, but someone who sits under bad sermons long enough will lose that ability.

It is easy to see how artists and composers are the preachers of general revelation if we think about how artists and composers work and then compare their work to sermon preparation. A composer comes up with a small melodic snippet that catches his imagination. He hears in those few notes the potential for development, involving perhaps conflict and resolution. He builds a framework lasting many minutes, during which that snippet can relate to itself and perhaps to other antagonistic snippets to create a musical narrative. The painter, likewise, passes by a fruit bowl lit by the morning sun as it sends a narrow beam through the kitchen window. He stops in front of it because, in that fruit bowl, a host of interrelated shapes and colors play with one another, coming to life in the limited light that exposes them. He decides on a particular vantage point because he wants to capture just those relationships apparent there. He exaggerates some details and glosses over others, so that we will notice just the things he notices and be moved by just the things that move him. And what is it that moves him? The invisible attributes of God, of course, made known in the things that are made. Anyone who has prepared a sermon can see the parallels: one comes to the biblical text and examines it; one looks for connections within the ideas there, as well as for what those ideas tell us about other things in Scripture; and then one writes a sermon that focuses on those connections to help the congregation better understand them—and thereby understand God.

Incidentally, the preacher and the artist are, as much as the bowl of fruit, "things that have been made." So the preacher himself, like the pomegranate, is an example of general revelation. His very ability to tell us about God's Word tells us something about God, which brings us to the next reason for enjoying fine arts.

REASON 2: ART AND MUSIC ARE COMMUNICATION FROM OUR FELLOW MAN

To have the God of the universe speak to you is no small thing. It is only through this that we will have life and health and peace. We know that God speaks through the Bible. But that same Bible tells us that God speaks through his creation too. How is it, for instance, that the meadows and valleys of Psalm 65:13 "shout and sing together for joy" except through the way they look? Or how is it that in Psalm 148 the sea creatures and deeps and fire and hail and snow and mist and all the other things there listed are to praise the Lord? They can only do so by their forms, since they have no other language. We know that God speaks through design as well as through words. So do artists and composers.

One of the pleasures of looking at a painting is that of receiving communication from another human—one who articulates the relationships between visual objects that we've never thought of and articulates them more clearly than we could. Through the artist's design, we learn about the nature of design itself, but, almost as interesting, we learn *from* someone else. The postmodern rightly questions this possibility. He wonders how it is we can be so confident that we understand what the artist or composer is getting at. "How do I know that I understand what my neighbor has said to me?" The Christian faith answers, "Because God's glory is made known *through* the very process of communication (Gen. 2:19; Acts 2:3). Since God is zealous for his glory (John 16:14), we know that he will uphold communication inasmuch as it gives him glory (though, see Genesis 11)." So while we *can* misunderstand one another as easily in art and music as we can in conversation and gesture, this potential for misunderstanding is routinely overcome, in a conversation as in a concerto, by the intervening work of God's common grace. Consequently, when we look at a Constable landscape, we learn about the design of landscape from someone better at observing that design than we and in the process have a conversation that reaches across history.

This brings with it an improved historical imagination for the viewer. Painting can help us to understand God through his providence in history. Some people treat art as if this were its main purpose, so that, one must suppose, the great painters took up their work like the soccer mom with her video recorder—because a record of the event *must* be made for posterity. But this is not principally why painters paint, so it is not principally on this ground that we should engage the message of their painting. Painters paint because they have something to say through design. Because God upholds human conversation, we can listen. And we enjoy learning what the world can look like through the eyes of another.[2]

REASON 3: ART AND MUSIC HELP US AVOID BEING DESENSITIZED

A student, during a class discussion about a still-life painting, remarks that "the artist has randomly arranged an equally random selection of fruits and vegetables." In a discussion about a fiery piano etude, an otherwise bright student exclaims that "the piece is just random chords banged out as loudly as possible." The students can use the word *random* because of the intuitive but false assumption that the making of art and music is an impulsive act— that the things to be found there might appear without any more effort from the artist than the effort he might exert to bring up a freckle on his own cheek. And, to be fair to the students, the

---

[2] C. S. Lewis, *An Experiment in Criticism* (Cambridge, UK: Cambridge University Press, 1961), epilogue.

word *random* could be applied correctly to art or music were they dreadfully bad. A careless artist might make a slip with his brush and give us designs resulting from biomechanics rather than from human reason. Although there was no such "slip of the brush" in the incidents described above, one can appreciate why the students suspected randomness in forms they did not understand. But what if the artist were inerrant?

Consider the observer of an oak tree who notes that "its branches jut out all at random." Or consider the fisherman who says he enjoys the view of his pond because of "its random clusters of lily pads." As soon as one believes in the God of the Bible, who gave to the wind its weight, to the waters their measure, to the lightning its way (Job 28:24–27), and to the sparrow the time of its demise (Matt. 10:29), one must believe that the growth patterns of an oak tree or the drift of lily pads must be the result of his will, too. This means that the look of the natural world (to say nothing of its fitness or function) is no more random than the letters inside the copy of Scripture at your bedside. Both are messages to us, and we do well to learn their languages.

But our culture is not very sensitive to the language of the natural world. Offer a room full of average, TV-watching, iPod-listening, text-messaging people a box of crayons and ask them to select a color for the trunk of an oak tree. Most of them will select the brown crayon, though the trunk is gray. Hum a tune to them in major mode (the musical mode of "Happy Birthday to You" and "Jesus Loves the Little Children") and then hum the same tune turned to minor mode (the musical mode of "When Johnny Comes Marching Home Again" and "God Rest You Merry, Gentlemen"). Then quiz them for ten minutes, moving back and forth from one version of the tune to another and asking which is major and which is minor. More will get the answers wrong than will get them right. Yet, the difference between gray and brown and between major and minor mode are not subtle ones. For a culinary example, consider the offerings of candy in the chrome-and-glass vending machines at the exits of your average big-box store. Many are marked with words that sound like threats: "atomic warhead," "tear-jerker" or "super sour." (Can any reader remember the day when the word "sour" was applied to foods that had gone bad?) Go to the toiletries section and, where years ago delicate scents like lavender and bluebells once sat, you'll find overwhelmingly acrid ones instead, often named after implements of physical trauma.

It seems that our culture sees the world only in the colors of plastic toys, hears from it only low thuds (consider the recent rise in sales of sub-woofers for home theaters), tastes only when the tongue is etched by acid, and smells only acrid chemicals. But if God is revealing himself to us in the things he has made, and if we as a culture are becoming less and less sensitive, then we will less and less understand God as he is revealed generally. Hundreds of years ago, the church began a campaign to make the world literate so that it could read God's Word. Perhaps we need another campaign to make the world sensitive so that it can "read" God's works. It is almost as if the Devil, having tried to deceive us of the truth of God's glory for millennia, has now changed his tactics and tries to get us to gouge out our own eyes and stop up our ears—or rather, to benumb our own intellects to the point that neither eyes nor ears will do us any good. Art and music can offer us a recovery from this illness because artists and musicians, gifted as they are in attending to the beauty of creation, help us through their own designs to attend to that beauty as well. Their expressions, far from random, help us understand the subtleties in the designs of nature that our blindness overlooked as randomness.

REASON 4: FAILURE TO ENJOY ART AND MUSIC INVITES FOLLY

In an essay about having "eyes to see," C. S. Lewis describes the process of avoiding God thus:

The avoiding, in many times and places, has proved so difficult that a very large part of the human race failed to achieve it. But in our own time and place it is extremely easy. Avoid silence, avoid solitude, avoid any train of thought that leads off the beaten track. Concentrate on money, sex, status, health and (above all) on your own grievances. Keep the radio on. Live in a crowd. Use plenty of sedation. If you must read books, select them very carefully. But you'd be safer to stick to the papers. You'll find the advertisements helpful; especially those with a sexy or snobbish appeal.[3]

The commonality in all the items on Lewis's list is not that they are all things that lie, but that they are all things that prohibit both truth and lies from being contemplated. The reason why the radio (in Lewis's day much less noxious than our own) can keep a man from God is not that he will likely hear pornographic songs there (though he will) but that those pornographic songs don't even invite enough intellectual clarity from the listener to allow him to idolize sexuality well. Were they to do even this much, he might awaken to a hope for something better. As discussed in chapter 1, beauty is the medium for truth. If a work of art is beautiful, it will allow truths to be communicated with clarity. If we avoid the things that speak most clearly—like great art and music—we avoid the opportunity to contemplate the truth. "The wise lay up knowledge," says Solomon (Prov. 10:14).

By "truth" we do not mean only the subject matter of a narrative painting or the text of a song. Of course, truth may be found there. But the peculiar success of art and music is that it brings to us a special species of truth that can be articulated only through visual or musical design. Indeed, there are works of art, like the pagan statuary of Greece, for which the subject matter is false but for which the design—that is, the message spoken by the form—is very true.

---

[3] "The Seeing Eye," first published in *Show* 3 (February 1963) under a title, "Onward, Christian Spacemen," that was odious to the author. Here cited from *C. S. Lewis: Essay Collection and Other Short Pieces*, ed. Lesley Walmsley (London: HarperCollins, 2000), 59.

What does it look like, then, to cut oneself off from these truths? We may see something of it in the life of Charles Darwin, who had the candor (or folly?) to report his own degeneration thus:

> Up to the age of thirty, or beyond it, poetry of many kinds, such as the works of Milton, Gray, Byron, Wordsworth, Coleridge, and Shelley, gave me great pleasure, and even as a schoolboy I took intense delight in Shakespeare, especially in the historical plays. I have also said that formerly pictures gave me considerable, and music very great delight. But now for many years I cannot endure to read a line of poetry; I have tried lately to read Shakespeare, and found it so intolerably dull that it nauseated me. I have also almost lost my taste for pictures or music. . . . I retain some taste for fine scenery, but it does not cause me the exquisite delight which it formerly did.[4]

Note that it is not merely the content of the poems, many of which had spiritual implications distasteful to Darwin, that bothered him. He could not endure even a "line" of poetry. Even "pictures" and "fine scenery" (that is, art and walks in nature) did little for the aged atheist. Romans 1:18–32 describes not a single instance or state of being, but a process. Notice that in verse 21 men "knew God," but then their thinking "became futile" and their hearts "were darkened." In verse 22, they "*became* fools." What were they before they became fools? Presumably, they were what Darwin was before he stopped liking Milton.

CONCLUSION

Ask a dozen Christians to fill in the blank from Genesis 1:10:

> God called the dry land Earth, and the waters that were gathered together he called Seas. And God _____ that it was good.

---

[4] Francis Darwin, ed., *The Life and Letters of Charles Darwin, Including an Autobiographical Chapter*, vol. 1 (London: John Murray, 1887), 100–101.

The chances are very great that a full half of the Christians you ask will fill in the blank with the word "said." We hear it thus misquoted even from the pulpit. No doubt, when a great artist steps back from a great work of art, he may in a moment of self-congratulation say, "Ah, a good one." But it is not his declaration that makes it so. Neither was it God's. The missing word is not "said" but "saw." God could not, without violating his own character, merely declare any old creation "good" by order of his word. He *saw* that it was already good; he needn't *say* anything to make it so. We are not told of a God who self-awards but of a God who contemplates. If God enjoys a bit of art appreciation at the end of a week of work, why should we deny ourselves the same pleasure?

Notice that God does not look back with fond memory on the formlessness that has now been displaced. He shows no regret for the lost deep over which he once brooded. Instead, he pauses to enjoy the most beautiful physical objects around. We follow his example when we elect to fill our leisure hours with the very best things we can—among which are the best works of art and music. Lamentably, many Christians justify their fondness for things nearly "without form and void" by trying to point out one or two good things in those leisure activities. "Sure, the pop song I like isn't as good as Beethoven, but there's more in it than you think." Yes, and there may have been something poignant about the earth without form and void, so pregnant with potential as it was. But this will be true of all created things, even the ones that humanity has, as far as possible, muted. We are to pursue the *best* things.

3

HOW DO WE JUDGE ART AND MUSIC?

Having ended the previous chapter with a call to pursue the best things, it's only fair that we discuss at this point how one identifies the best things so as to pursue them. One encounters a bewildering array of recommendations. Charlie Brown's friend Schroeder likes Beethoven. Bill Clinton likes Fleetwood Mac. One's roommate swears by a band called Panic! at the Disco. Most bewildering of all is the consistent dichotomy between what is highly regarded by experts and what is actually popular. According to *Billboard*, the American rapper Eminem was the most successful musician of the last decade, but his work rarely appears in the curricula of university music departments. Something like one in twenty American homes contains a Thomas Kinkade painting. Why, then, does not a single major museum? Musicologist Joseph Kerman compares listening to Beethoven's String Quartet in F Major, Op. 59, No. 1, to a trip to Athens or a first kiss. You would think many would be drawn to such pleasure. And, yet, do you person- ally know anyone who is? Anyone who listens to this quartet for pleasure? The dichotomy is so striking that we naturally want to understand it better.

Adherents to the classical view of beauty have an explanation: the masses are too stupid to recognize how to get what they want. The classicist thinks he knows why ordinary people include art and music in their lives, and he has developed all sorts of rules

47

for pleasing them. But, again and again, people don't seem to be particularly moved by the results of his rules. And, again and again, he has to bend his rules to explain why certain unclassical works deserve a place in his *canon* (his authoritative list of approved works). What does a classicist do, for example, with the titanic asymmetry and sweeping transformations of the Beethoven quartet just mentioned? He cannot, with a neo-Aristotelian formula, explain the delight he takes in them. And there are other even more embarrassing problems with the classicist's typical take on the dichotomy (that is, the dichotomy between the tastes of the few who love highbrow things and the tastes of the many who do not). "Some critics write of those who constitute the literary 'many' as if they belonged to the many in every respect, and indeed to the rabble," wrote C. S. Lewis.

> They accuse them of illiteracy, barbarism, "crass," "crude" and "stock" responses which (it is suggested) must make them clumsy and insensitive in all the relations of life and render them a permanent danger to civilisation. It sometimes sounds as if the reading of "popular" fiction involved moral turpitude [depravity]. I do not find this borne out by experience. I have a notion that these "many" include certain people who are equal or superior to some of the few in psychological health, in moral virtue, practical prudence, good manners, and general adaptability. And we all know very well that we, the literary, include no small percentage of the ignorant, the caddish, the stunted, the warped, and the truculent. With the hasty and wholesale *apartheid* of those who ignore this we must have nothing to do.[1]

We know members of both groups too well to be convinced by any explanation of the difference between them based on differences in moral character or intellect.

Postmoderns look for a political explanation. Perhaps the works of art and music in the college syllabus are there because

---

[1] C. S. Lewis, *An Experiment in Criticism* (Cambridge, UK: Cambridge University Press, 1961), 5–6.

powerful people prefer those works and are in a position to foist their tastes on students. If I hold a relativist mind-set, I do not study a Houdon bust or a Brahms intermezzo because Houdon or Brahms have some wisdom to share with me, which I will be happier for having encountered. At most, I study them as historical artifacts—evidence of how Houdon and Brahms manipulated people to reinforce social systems that were advantageous to Houdon and Brahms. After all, if every claim to beauty is equally valid, then there can be no grounds for including some works in a syllabus and excluding others, other than historical curiosity and a sense of representational fairness.

Those who subscribe to the historic Christian view of beauty, however, think they have a more plausible explanation for the difference between great art and popular art. In chapter 1 we argued that something is beautiful when its form realizes a good purpose. If people differ in their purposes for looking at art or listening to music, it follows that they will be attracted to different kinds of art and music, according to the forms that best realize their purposes. And it's evident that people *do* have different purposes—various, good purposes—for art and music. So only a foolish critic tries to judge the absolute worth of a piece apart from questions of purpose. One smiles to think what impression Gregorian chant would make if a DJ played some at a dance; this does not in the least lessen the value of Gregorian chant for another purpose. Likewise, a parent trying to soothe a tired baby would be foolish to use a military march. The planner of a funeral would be foolish to hire a polka band. And if you need background music at a party, don't select an opera.

Is it possible, then, that Schroeder and Mr. Clinton like different music because they have different purposes for their music? Might the few mean one thing by the word *like* (when they say they "like" great art) and the many mean something else entirely (when they say they "like" popular art)? This is the hypothesis tested in

C. S. Lewis's *An Experiment in Criticism* (1961), a book that we, the authors of this volume, consider the most compelling of all explanations of artistic greatness. It is worthy of a summary.

USE AND RECEPTION

Although *An Experiment in Criticism* is ostensibly about literary criticism, its arguments apply to all of life, including art and music. (In fact, the book includes a chapter called "How the Few and the Many Use Pictures and Music.") Why, Lewis asks, do the few, who appreciate great books, read them repeatedly? Why do they prize them so dearly, "always looking for leisure and silence in which to read and do so with their whole attention"?

He gets at an answer by distinguishing two ways of reading. The many, who appreciate popular books, seem to *use* them for their own *preconceived* purposes. They desire the sensations of narrative excitement, say, (or of suspense, or of vicarious happiness) and—understandably—seek out books that will satisfy this desire as efficiently as possible, with a minimum of expense and distraction.

The few, who appreciate great books, may desire these sensations, too. In contrast with the many, however, they also desire something more: they wish to *receive*. Not just fulfilling their preconceived purposes, they wish through books to discover new purposes for books—new to them, that is—purposes they cannot anticipate. They are looking for books that will provide pleasures they do not yet desire because they cannot know anything about them before encountering them in the books. Defined in this way, it's easy to see why receivers cherish reception; it is a kind of grace, really—a blessing we cannot seek on our own because we don't even know we need it until the book shows us that we do.

Most people go through life using pictures. A college student may buy a poster with his hard-earned money, devote scarce wall space in his dorm room to it, and feel perfectly satisfied with the poster, and yet derive this satisfaction *not from looking at it* but from displaying it and using what is represented there as an aid to his own mental activities. He hangs up a picture of a pretty girl because he likes to be reminded of pretty girls. That doesn't mean he is prepared to appreciate the peculiar beauties of this particular girl (assuming there is a licit way to do so, without lust); in fact, the more peculiar a girl's beauty, the less likely it is that she will appear in his poster. Perhaps the student hangs up a political poster because he wants to make a statement to visitors. Or he hangs up a poster of a commercial product because he's pleased to associate with that product. But the more the poster actually says about the girl or politics or the commercial product through color, line, shape, and composition—that is, the more pictorially communicative it is—the less pleased the student will be, because such communication is an impediment to his use. He is interested in the meaning he reads into the poster, not in what the poster itself means. This is in contrast to the "few" who discover new wonders daily in their posters and may even shed a tear of joy over the discovery. The many, should they visit an art museum, flit from work to work in an effort to get their money's worth, while the few spend their time in front of just three paintings—maybe forty minutes on each—and leave exhausted but exhilarated by what they have seen.

Or imagine two songs sharing the same subject matter, written with different kinds of listeners in mind. One kind of listener looks for forms that will powerfully confirm what he already knows. He is pleased by the familiar, by what stimulates without asking anything of him, by what offers the sensations of an active emotional life without the difficulty that normally goes along with one. He expects his aesthetic experiences to be immediate and disposable. He has some use for his music: to soothe his nerves, to propel his body in the dance, to provide a corporate identity for his group, or to divert him during his commute to work. The other kind of listener looks for forms that reveal to him new ways of thinking, perspectives not his own. He is delighted by adventures that lead him far afield from what he already knows so that he might transcend his previously limited viewpoint and be enlarged. According to Lewis's hypothesis, the forms of popular culture tend to speak to the first kind of listening, while the forms of high culture tend to speak to the second kind of listening. (The forms of folk culture tend to do both. Genuine folk culture may now be only a feeble residue of what it once was, but wherever ordinary people still sing to one another, the form of the song can be "received" as a manifestation of a relationship. When Joe serenades Amber, it does not merely provide a vague reminder of the concept of love through which Joe and Amber can experience certain desirable feelings; it communicates *Joe's* love *for Amber.*)

Reception involves, first, "laying aside as completely as we can all our own preconceptions, interests, and associations" to make room for the artist's message. Then, "after the negative effort, the positive. We must use our eyes. We must look, and go on looking till we have certainly seen exactly what is there." The receiver is not passive. "His also is an imaginative activity; but an obedient one. He seems passive at first because he is making sure of his orders. If, when they have been fully grasped, he decides that they are not worth obeying—in other words, that this is a bad picture—he turns away altogether."[2]

Lewis summarizes the whole argument in what has become the most famous paragraph of the book:

> A work of (whatever) art can be either "received" or "used." When we "receive" it we exert our senses and imagination and various other powers according to a pattern invented by the artist. When we "use" it we treat it as assistance for our own activities. The one, to use an old-fashioned image, is like being taken

---

[2] Ibid., 18–20.

for a bicycle ride by a man who may know roads we have never yet explored. The other is like adding one of those little motor attachments to our own bicycle and then going for one of our familiar rides. These rides may in themselves be good, bad, or indifferent. The "uses" which the many make of the arts may or may not be intrinsically vulgar, depraved, or morbid. That's as may be. "Using" is inferior to "reception" because art, if used rather than received, merely facilitates, brightens, relieves or palliates our life, and does not add to it.[3]

Lewis calls the book *An Experiment* for a reason. He is making a scientific, not a moral, argument. Rather than trying to convince anyone to change reading habits, he merely seeks to explain a phenomenon (the dichotomy between great and popular books) that is not sufficiently accounted for in traditional literary criticism. He never claims that reception is better than use. It is *superior* in the sense that reception has more potential to enrich our lives, but it is not intrinsically good. Books can be put to good or bad uses. And that which we receive from books may be either good or bad. Consider a phone book. Its purpose is to facilitate the efficient and accurate retrieval of phone numbers. If its form realizes this purpose well, we say it is a beautiful phone book: its form admirably facilitates a good *use*. How senseless it would be to try to *receive* a phone book! On the other hand, anyone who tries to use *Paradise Lost* to satisfy a hankering for thrilling action will be frustrated. And woe betide anyone who tries to receive *Playboy*.

Lewis's book succeeds rhetorically because all happy people have learned to appreciate something in the way the few do. We also, each of us, know from constant firsthand experience what it means to use something in the way the many do. Some people play board games as a diversion; they use them as a medium for interacting with and competing with friends at leisure. But that's not all

[3] Ibid., 88.

board games mean; some have been deeply touched by the beauty of the game; they talk at length, to whoever will listen, about the physical textures and strategic layers of The Settlers of Catan; or for the rest of their lives they will mull over Bobby Fisher's gambit against Boris Spassky in 1972. Both of us admit that we use cars. We drive two of the ugliest and oldest cars in the college lot, content that they get us to and from work. Obviously we are missing something, because, as others will testify, a well-designed car is something to make the heart sing. Is it such a stretch to infer something similar in the hearts of those who appreciate great art and music?

The application of Lewis's hypothesis to the overarching question of this chapter is plain. How do we judge art and music? If he is correct, a work is ugly to the extent that its form realizes an evil purpose, whether it be an evil "use" or the "reception" of something evil. A work is also ugly to the extent that its form poorly realizes a good purpose, whether it be a good "use" or the "reception" of something good. Obversely, a work is beautiful if its form well realizes a good purpose. But we cannot correctly judge without knowing the purpose. It will not do to compare apples and oranges or to criticize a work for failing to do something it was never intended to.

AN ILLUSTRATION

But what, exactly, is received through great art and music? The descriptions above may seem conveniently vague. Yet when the "few" try to describe the particulars they have delighted in, the eyes of those around will, more often than not, glaze over. "Yes. Yes. But what does the painting *mean*?"

We knew a student from a densely populated major city who never had reason to travel from home until moving away to study. Her night sky had been so full of artificial light that she grew up without ever seeing a star (other than the sun, of course). For her, stars were something in books. To someone in this situation, it can be interesting to hear about light-years and ionized gas, but these things alone give little sense of the pleasures of stargazing. So, too, with any kind of reception. An attempt to describe it to the uninitiated may come across as only so much data.

Nevertheless, we shall try. We shall try to give some sense of what can be received from great art by comparing examples of a type of art that has been both widely used and widely received. The representation of Christ on the cross has historically been one of the most important genres in Western art. Countless places of worship have been decorated with one. And there it is *used* to direct the worshipers' thoughts and affections to the Savior's work of redemption. Such an image "had better not have any excellencies, subtleties, or originalities which will fix attention upon itself."[4] Crucifixes sold at a Catholic gift shop for use in churches, homes, and schools all look alike. They are "generic" in the common sense of the word. They say very little about what actually happened at Golgotha or what it meant. They say just enough to serve as a reminder of atonement: Jesus's body is partially naked, his arms extended, his hands and feet pierced, his head falling limp to one shoulder, and his eyes closed. Anything more, and it could be treated as an object worthy of contemplation in its own right, diverting attention from the real Jesus who is to be worshiped now in this place.

Pictures of the crucifixion that have made their way into art museums look very different. Before reading on, please find a full-color, high-definition reproduction of Matthias Grünewald's painting of the crucifixion from his Isenheim Altarpiece. (An Internet search for "Grünewald" and "Isenheim" or "Grünewald" and "Crucifixion" should do.) Then study it at length. What colors does Grünewald use in his painting? Why? How does he draw the figures? Why? How does he arrange the figures? Why?

---

[4]Ibid., 17.

Matthias Grünewald, *Crucifixion*, central panel of the closed Isenheim Altarpiece, ca.1510–1515. Oil on limewood panel, 299 x 327 cm. Musée d'Unterlinden, Colmar, France. Photo credit: Scala / Art Resource, NY.

Now that you have drawn some conclusions of your own, let's confer.

1) Every viewer is immediately assaulted by gruesome details of Jesus's physical suffering. His body has been violated in hundreds of ways, all carefully delineated by the painter. (Try to find a close-up reproduction of any part of Jesus's body.) It seems Grünewald was the Mel Gibson of the sixteenth century.

2) The figures are not drawn to scale. Since Christ's body is so much larger than the others', it appears to project out in front of the canvas, an effect augmented by the proximity (and immensity) of the rock face pushed right up against his calves. Grünewald gets in our face to confront us with Christ's misery.

3) Whereas most depictions of the crucifixion position Christ's body high above the earth and above the horizon, so that we look up at him and—by implication—to the heaven he won

for us, here Christ's body is positioned low and almost at the same level as the saints. The plane of our vision is at his thighs. The whole composition is earthbound. The beam of the cross seems to sag under the weight of the corpse.

4) The painting is wider than it is tall. Whereas most images of the crucifixion are vertical in orientation, this one is horizontal. The strong horizontal lines of the rock, the crossbeam, and the white sign check any vertical motion the picture might have, just as nails check the vertical reach of Christ's fingers. The vertical post is altogether lost in shadow.

5) Not just the vertical post, but all the background, is lost in shadow. We recall the sun failed at Christ's death, but this black is pitch.

6) Besides black, the only color of any intensity is the lurid red. Other colors, in addition to being washed out, appear in places they shouldn't: blue in Christ's lips, green in his feet, etc.

7) The saints arch back, as if recoiling in horror. John the Baptist comes closest to standing straight but only because his feet are planted so firmly; note the tautness of his muscles.

In short, the composite effect of all these elements of design, as they interact with the subject matter, is to communicate the ugliness of Christ's crucifixion. In history, this event was surely the ugliest ever, when the incarnate Son of God ceased to breathe. Speaking personally, I know the ugliest thing *I* have ever seen is my own sin, and that sin was imputed—along with every other sin committed by his people against the infinite holiness of God—to Christ on the cross. He who knew no sin was made to "be sin" (2 Cor. 5:21), the penalty for which seems unbearable. By exaggerating his physical agony, Grünewald develops a visible metaphor for Christ's spiritual agony.

When a theologian says, "Christ underwent the pains of hell so we wouldn't have to," it is a good and proper thing to say, and we need to hear theologians say it. But when they do, are they really saying the same thing Grünewald does? Or, rather, are some kinds of knowledge necessarily visual? Even if the painter can't say as much as the wordsmith does, and even if what he says isn't as important, aren't we better off for having both?[5] We are seeing-creatures who inhabit a visible world, and as such we cannot escape the fact that some kinds of knowledge come to us by sight. In any case, although it takes time for the viewer to process, there's plainly a surplus of meaning in Grünewald's painting. It could never succeed as a mere reminder of the atonement. It defies use.

Before continuing, please find and study a full-color, high-definition reproduction of Raphael's *Mond Crucifixion* (we recommend the website of the National Gallery in London). Again, ask yourself as many questions as possible about how this painting communicates through color, line, shape, and composition.

We have chosen to illustrate the possibility of reception by comparing these two paintings because they have the same subject matter—the same people doing the same things. The paintings also happen to have been made only about a decade apart. Any difference in message must come from differences in the *design* of the painting—the very thing users are least attentive to.

---

[5] Some readers, while agreeing in principle that it's a blessing to receive pictures as well as words, may deny it in this instance, since this is a picture of the second person of the godhead, which they believe to be outlawed by the second commandment. This book intentionally sidesteps their concerns. It is enough for the argument here to admit that some kinds of knowledge come to us by sight. We do not, by this expedient, pretend that the second commandment or the debate surrounding it, is unimportant. Christians range in their application of this commandment from the veneration of images of all three persons of the Trinity in posture, word, and thought in corporate and private worship (as is the case in Eastern Orthodoxy) to the prohibition of any representation of any of the persons of the Trinity in any way or context (as is the case with some forms of Reformed Protestantism). Only, this debate is not the one taken up in this volume.

Raphael, *The Mond Crucifixion*, 1502–1503. Oil on poplar, 28.3 x 167.3 cm. ©National Gallery, London / Art Resource, NY.

In studying the Raphael you may have noticed the following.

1) The figures are lovely. Christ, especially, is perfect, like some Greek heroic statue.

2) In contrast to Grünewald's distortions, part of what makes Christ so lovely here is that Raphael draws him in due proportion to the other humans. (The dancing angels, being nonhuman creatures from another world, are drawn to some other scale.)

3) Christ's body is elevated, separating the picture into two halves. We look up.

4) The painting has a vertical orientation.

5) The painting is filled with bright, serene light. We can see far into a park-like landscape that recedes through a rational color scheme of yellow transitioning through green to blue. All creation, including angels, sun, and moon, witnesses Christ's work.

6) The colors are many and balanced, with just the right amounts of azure, navy, green, yellow, red, lavender, and pink, so that no colors outweigh others. Although the navy blue traditionally worn by Jesus's mother, Mary, is perhaps the least likely to attract notice, she still figures prominently because the lines and illumination of the landscape behind her counteract the power of John's ruby red and Mary Magdalene's pink to steal our attention. The slope of the hill repeatedly directs us back to the mother, who calmly returns our gaze.

7) The worshiping saints and angels are arranged symmetrically in a large diamond shape that, by complementing the symmetries of cross and earth and sky, contributes to the overall sense of balance and harmony.

These things communicate the beauty of the most beautiful event in history, when the goodness and mercy of God were most clearly glorified. There is no contradiction in using both superlatives—most ugly and most beautiful—here, for the cross lies at the very center of Christian aesthetics. Just as the sin of believers was imputed to the Lord Jesus, so his righteousness was imputed to them. When they fix their gaze on the cross in faith, they, like the kneeling figures of St. Jerome and Mary Magdalene, are sanctified in the beauty of holiness. And, as observed with the Grünewald, these ideas can be communicated visually to complement and not duplicate verbal proclamation.

CONCLUSION

The reason partakers of popular culture and high culture are mystified by each other's tastes is that they apply entirely different criteria for judging culture, according to whether they are accustomed to using it or receiving it. There are many appropriate *uses* for art and music, which need not be denigrated. But for the leisurely contemplation of general revelation,[6] for what we do when we listen to (as opposed to "put on") music and look at (as opposed to "put up") art, the best works will be those that, like the Grünewald and the Raphael, reward *reception*.

---

[6] See chap. 2 in this volume.

✚ 4

LOOKING AT ART

The most important part of looking at art is looking at art. Go to any major gallery and you'll see how many people seem unaware of this. A good number of them will be in conversation with friends—conversation of a sort that forbids attention to anything beyond that conversation. Some will be taking blurry pictures of friends in front of great art. Others will have their noses in the gallery guide, reading about the biographies of artists whose biographies are only interesting because of the art they produced—which is in that very gallery! Some will be reading the plastic placards beside the art, admitting that they would rather have someone else look at the art and then provide them with a summary of it. Many will hide out in the gift shop, since shopping is more customary than looking at art. But the number of people actually looking at art will be pretty small. These individuals stand out awkwardly. If the crowd is especially large, and bovine tendencies are encouraged in it by means of red velvet ropes and timed audio-guides, these individuals will receive the mild scorn of other gallery goers—they interrupt the path of the herd. One has the overwhelming urge to say, in a voice audible above the din, "Don't forget to look," just as some exercise instructors say, not without cause, "Don't forget to breathe."

One of the advantages of a Christian aesthetic is that it gives us motivation to overcome our spiritual and cultural tendencies and actually look at art. Once we know that it is one corner of God's glory that we evade when we look at an inscribed plastic placard instead of a Rembrandt, we find ourselves compelled to be one of the awkward few who stand in front of the paintings. The work we do there—the intellectual labor of noticing relationships between color and shape, the work of following line to objects of importance, the thoughtful engagement with subject matter—is not easy. But neither is it foreign to us. For though to read a book in Latin requires special training in a language we do not learn from birth, "reading" a work of art requires familiarity with a language that everyone of all eras learns from birth. Blood ran just as red and grass grew just as green in fifteenth-century Flanders as it does today, so red and green say many of the same things to us as to a painter of the Northern Renaissance. Eyes still gravitate toward light and strain at darkness, both in seventeenth-century Holland and in twenty-first-century America. Art of all ages can speak to all ages through its most art-like mode of utterance. Sure, subject matters have changed. We do not understand the dress and manners of older ages as well as we understand our own. We are not as familiar with classical mythology or the lives of the saints as were those who lived before us. But these are only one part of the meaning of great works. This is why art is accessible even to the uninitiated and sometimes even the very young. While historical imagination and familiarity with the broader subjects of Western civilization will very much enrich the experience of art appreciation, it is not as essential as merely looking at the art.

On that note, we urge readers to place a slip of paper in the book at this page and then find large, color reproductions of Rogier van der Weyden's *Deposition*, Pieter Claesz's *Still Life with Turkey Pie*, and Makoto Fujimura's *Golden Countenance*. Spend about fifteen minutes with each of the three paintings. Try to notice what the image seems to ask you to notice and then return to read the corresponding portion of this chapter. If for whatever reason you cannot do this now, do not read on, for what follows will surely be nonsense until you have taken a look at these images.

Rogier van der Weyden, *Deposition*, ca. 1436. Oil on wood, 220 x 262 cm. Museo del Prado, Madrid, Spain. Photo Credit: Scala / Art Resource, NY.

COMPLICATED GRIEF:
ROGIER VAN DER WEYDEN'S *DEPOSITION*

Rogier van der Weyden's *Deposition* is a painting about grief over Christ's death. Put as simply as that, you would think it might be a simple painting. The Christian knows, however, that grief over Christ's death is a complicated thing—it leads to our joy—and a good painting that is to treat such a topic will be as rich in meaning as the subject requires it to be. Rogier makes sure that we have no alternative but to meet the cold reality of Christ's death; he situates Christ's bleeding corpse on a diagonal that runs against the basic orientation of the panel. Christ's stark nudity, accentuated by a stream of runny blood that traces beneath his semitransparent loincloth, draws our attention even more than his placement. Indeed, the whole scene thrusts itself upon the viewer, with nothing in the background to distract us.

The arrangement of the figures is poignantly artificial. Here are four examples of the artifice: (1) Every figure to the left of the cross is balanced by a figure to the right so that, for example, Nicodemus (the figure with the red hat) adopts a gesture that is mirrored by the servant on the ladder above him. Joseph of Arimathea (just to the right the cross, in a gold embroidered gown) adopts the same posture as Mary Salome (in green, to the left of the cross). The other figures all have their visual counterparts. (2) Color likewise balances across the center line of the cross so that, for instance, the red of John the Beloved (who supports the Virgin Mary) can be found in the sleeves of Mary Magdalene (extreme right). Even Joseph's sumptuous coat is echoed in the garment behind the Virgin Mary. (3) The most prominent organizational feature is fittingly found in the forms of Christ and Mary. Mary's posture and gesture echo Christ's. (4) But their mutual gesture, of extended arms, is to be found in all figures excepting the ones on the extreme left and right. There we find two quite different gestures—Mary of Clopas embraces herself and cries bitterly while Mary Magdalene wrings her hands.

These are works of artifice. Here are the reasons why they are poignant:

1) Because the figures are balanced on either side of the vertical beam of the cross, the cross of Christ becomes the organizational home base. We move from one side of it to the other as we look at the image because eyes naturally move from like things to like things. This also causes us to trace the body of Christ, which is situated roughly in the middle of the cross. When we do both of these things together, we think on the reality of Christ's death and the instrument by which it was accomplished. The body is, as mentioned above, emphasized by its nudity, its gore, and its orientation.

2) The repeated bold colors serve the same purpose—to call our attention from one side of the cross to the other. The very restlessness of our eyes in the image is a good metaphor for the

restlessness of the disciples in the face of Christ's death and, ultimately, the restlessness of our own souls as we contemplate what that death means. The Son of God dies, but through that death we live.

3) Mary's body echoes Christ's because, as Simeon said to Mary, "a sword will pierce through your own soul also" (Luke 2:35). The staunchest Protestant needn't begrudge Rogier this gesture. But in Rogier's pre-Reformation Flanders it would remind viewers of the necessity of Mary's intercession to Christ and the interconnectedness of the two. The alignment of their hands creates an implied diagonal running perpendicular to that of their bodies, from Joseph of Arimathea's face through a golden space and Jesus's navel, along Nicodemus's right leg, through Mary's womb and John's left foot, to the skull that speaks of Golgotha and death. Above, an isosceles triangle formed by three heads (those of Mary of Clopas, John, and Mary Salome) points to the same spot—where the Virgin's hand almost touches the skull.

4) The extended, but therefore open, arms of Mary and Christ are an invitation to viewers and echoed by every other figure, excepting Mary of Clopas and Mary Magdalene. In Mary of Clopas, the open gesture of all the other figures finds its natural conclusion in an embrace—the wild arms of initial grief close in to gird her torso as she weeps. In Mary Magdalene, the open gestures of the other figures close prematurely, and interlocked hands turn out, inflicting pain that distracts from the internal grief. Magdalene, the figure of Christian penance for the Middle Ages, is here penitent too. And her penitence is situated directly above the feet that she anointed at the time of her conversion (medievals identified Mary Magdalene with the "sinful woman" of Luke 7). The ointment is brought to mind by the white jar carried by Joseph's servant, situated also just beside Magdalene's hands.

But these designs are not the only ones to clarify our thoughts about the grief at the cross. The scene is set in a gilded box in imitation of the settings for sculpted wood figures in altarpieces of Rogier's day. Such a setting would have evoked in the viewer a sense of the supernatural, but the naturalistic figures evoke the natural. "Tis mystery all. Th'immortal dies." But this combination of immortal and mortal is to be found in the relationship between Christ and Mary, too. Mary is mortal yet brings into the world a divine son. Christ is divine, yet is born of a mortal because he is also mortal.

Because the relationship between Christ and Mary is so important to the ideas of the painting, we see it affecting not only those two figures, as in (3) above, but the others as well. Joseph's gaze passes through Christ's hands to Mary's and finally the skull. John's gaze is fixed on the point of contact between mother and son. The bright red hose on Nicodemus's legs draw our attention, and especially so because of their uncomfortable angles, to the two protagonists. His left leg intersects with Christ's right hip, and his right leg intersects with Mary's left hip. Though it is Christ who has died, Mary is the one who seems to be lowered into the ground. John and Mary Salome hold the Virgin Mother suspended at knee level, while Nicodemus holds Christ tight at almost chest level. The result is surprising. The Virgin Mother seems to descend down from the group of three figures behind her while Christ seems to fly up from Joseph's knees. Since Christ's body is neither up nor down, it can take on a buoyancy that, notwithstanding the limp neck, makes it seem ready to rise. The inverted triangle formed by the three heads above the Virgin invites us to see the corresponding three heads on the right side of the painting as another, if much flatter, triangle. Its base (the inclined heads of Joseph and Magdalene) runs parallel to the bodies of Jesus and the Virgin, and its apex points up and away in the same direction as Magdalene's pleading hands, hinting at hope and ascent.

Indeed, Christ's body shows life and death together in one form. His face is dead, with half-open mouth and lifeless eyes. But the veins in his arms still bulge. His skin wears a pallor that is not normal, but compare it to the skin of the coarse Roman servant at the top of the ladder. An objective look will judge the rustic more pallid than Christ. (Notice that the Roman servant is the only one that takes the liberty to touch Christ's body with his bare hand.) The true look of death has been reserved exclusively for the Virgin Mary, who not only has colorless skin but colorless lips to match.

It takes almost no imagination to see what Rogier is after here. He is showing us the dual natures of Christ's death. The holy and the fleshly combine here. The hysterical-in-grief shares a scene with the thoughtful and brooding. The ascending spirit is implied alongside the descending body. The utterly predictable balanced composition is opposed by the contorted positions of Christ's neck, Nicodemus's legs, and Mary Magdalene's whole upper body, just as the utterly predictable executions of providence are sometimes bitter. The glamorous beauty of the figures is offset by their sorrowful brows. They are saints, but they are also subject to heartrending grief. The God bearer (*theotokos*) is also a mom.

By all this Rogier helps us to think about the right mix of emotions that come when we contemplate Christ's death. We know that our grief is ultimately limited by the reality of the resurrection (here evoked by the lifelike body, its ascendant posture, and the upward-pointing group of heads). But this does not change our sorrow (here explained through grief-stricken postures and expressions, through the Virgin's swoon, through Christ's dead face, and the downward-pointing group of heads) that such a thing came about because of our sin.

"TASTE AND SEE THAT THE LORD IS GOOD": PIETER CLAESZ'S *STILL LIFE WITH TURKEY PIE*

Rogier's painting finds a ready audience among modern Christians who are comfortable both with the theology of Christ's death and with images that convey a narrative. But still-life painting is harder because it conveys almost no narrative or theology directly. Sure, some still-life paintings may combine objects whose association suggests a gentle moral (like a skull and hourglass suggesting the inevitability of death). Some may represent a scene connected to an event (such as a meal or a hunt). But most of them have as their main purpose faithfully to represent beautiful objects that are combined in a beautiful way. If you've ever caught yourself looking at the way light refracts in a glass saltshaker or noticing the opalescence of a McIntosh apple peel, you have looked at an object in the way a still-life painter looks at it. You are no longer thinking of a seasoning to shake on your rice or keeping the doctor away but of the appearance—the glorious appearance—of God's creation.

Pieter Claesz, *Still Life with Turkey Pie*, 1627. Oil on board, 4' 3" × 2' 6". Photo credit: Rijksmuseum, Amsterdam.

The part of creation most likely to surprise modern viewers in this still life is the remains of a large dead turkey posed atop the turkey pie: head, neck, wings, and tail. In our own antiseptic culture, presenting food in this way seems distasteful or even grotesque. If we are honest, however, we must admit that it is more congruent than the aimless squiggles of red sauce we find on our plates at a fancy Manhattan restaurant. It solves a problem commonly encountered with pies when at first glance one wonders what has been baked in them. Remembering that turkey had been domesticated in Europe for only about a hundred years at this point, Tom is to be taken as a guest of honor at the feast. So important is he that he is a sort of vice-moderator of the image's composition. The moderator, the banqueter himself, is missing. The table is placed asymmetrically within the frame of the picture to reveal an empty space to the left of the table toward which several objects direct our attention, including the knife (which bears Claesz's signature), the spoon (still holding half a mouthful of pie), and the shadow of the wineglass. Even the turkey faces there, rose in beak, perhaps comically eying his absent predator who may once have sat across from him.

But while the banqueter is missing, we find, perhaps in front of his place, a pewter pot with a dog-headed spout that mocks the turkey that looks in its direction. Indeed, there are other forces that draw our eye to this pot. It sits at the end of a diagonal line created by the plates and is isolated in the left mid-ground. The pot reflects, in its convex body, the part of the room that is behind us—including the window that is the light source. The spout's "mirroring" of the turkey's posture parodies the pot's real mirroring of the whole room.

And so, in absence of the banqueter, the pot and the turkey relate to one another and thereby solicit the attentions of many of the remaining objects. The exquisite nautilus-shell vessel turns its brim up toward the turkey as if to offer it a libation. Does the fruit bowl turn toward the turkey or toward the pot? It is hard to say, but because of its angle we turn back from it toward the left to consider the smaller, sweet pie, partially consumed, in which we see a slice of citrus, a berry, and what may be a nut-based filling (see detail).

Claesz, *Still Life*, detail: smaller, sweet pie, partially consumed.

This invites connections between the fruit in the pie and the fruit in the bowl to the right and fruit on the plate in front. The nuts are not denied compatriots at the banquet either. The table is strewn with them, both cracked and uncracked. Indeed, the relation between opened and unopened objects is an important theme of this visual banquet. Below Tom, the pie, bread, oysters, and fruit bowl cluster into a group of whole objects, surrounded by their opened counterparts.

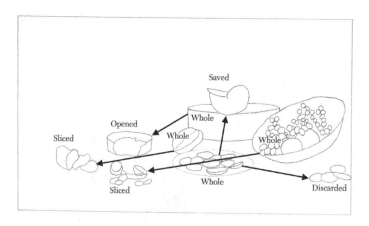

Claesz, *Still Life*, line diagram

The line diagram we have drawn may help get you started seeing these relationships, but keep going. Not only does Claesz show us fruit that is baked (pie) and fruit that is peeled (lemon) but also fruit that is sectioned (orange). The form of the orange section (below the plate of oysters) inverts the form of the scored loaf (above the plate); that is, it resembles the "missing" part of the otherwise ovoid-shaped loaf. Above the discarded oyster shells, we find a loaf of bread propping up the fruit bowl and hiding in its shadow. This is a larger version of the loaf we find in the center of the image. In the left above the peeled lemon, we find a sliced loaf, which we compare to the lemon because they are both sliced (see details).

Claesz, *Still Life*, details: sliced loaf, sliced lemon.

Perhaps the quietest participants in the table are the olives, tucked away in the background. But they are nevertheless important. For a start, the wall behind the table takes their color. The glass beside them does too, and the ornamental protrusions around its stem share their shape. These are not the only things that share their shape, however. Most of the objects here do. The grapes are ovular just like the olives. And so would the lemon be, were it whole. The nautilus too implies an oval with a section removed. The loaves of bread, both whole and cut, also suggest the shape of an oval. Even the plates, circular though they are, appear as ovals, thanks to our lowered vantage point.

A common response to an image like this is, "Yes, but what does it all mean?" The only answer to this question is to be found in something like what we have written in the previous three paragraphs. This *is* the meaning of the work, which is the same sort of meaning we find in creation all the time. If this does not satisfy, if we prefer Rogier's theology to Claesz's turkey, we should consider whether one of the reasons we are grateful for Christ's reconciling us to God through his death is that we know God is good. And we know he is good, in small part, because of turkey pie.

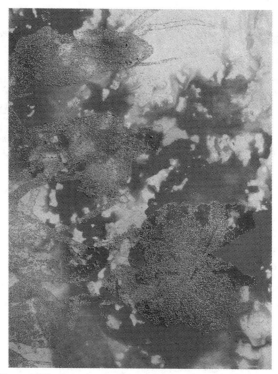

Makoto Fujimura, *Golden Countenance*, 2005. Ground mineral pigments on Kumohada paper, digital photograph by Ryann Cooley. Original in private collection. Photo credit: http://byfor.org and http://makotofujimura.com.

A STUDY OF RED THROUGH GOLD:
MAKOTO FUJIMURA'S *GOLDEN COUNTENANCE*

Abstract art should not pose a problem for anyone who can enjoy a still life like the one we have just studied. It should be an easy transition from a painting in which the subject matter is chosen based on its color and shape (as opposed to some narrative meaning) to a painting in which the subject matter is color and shape itself. But there is something unsettling about this transition. Abstract design itself isn't unsettling. We learn to enjoy it from the very first time we are allowed to pick out our own clothes and keep enjoying it even when we reach the age when we can pick out tile for our kitchen floor. When we meet abstract design in painting or sculpture, however, we are naturally resistant because we have come to expect painting and sculpture to be pictures *of* things. Not to worry. Makoto Fujimura's *Golden Countenance* is, like all abstract art, a picture *of* something too. This "something" is composition, color, and line.

The image is laid out with gold in the foreground. The gold he uses here has a grainy texture and sits on the surface like dust on the surface of a pond. The gold dust has congregated in the left side of the image, in four large groups or masses, the fourth of which extends past the left margin of the image, giving the viewer the sense that the ideas present here go on beyond his sight. In shape and size, each expanse of gold bears a resemblance to another, the top two expanses pairing off in a vertical alignment and the bottom two expanses in a horizontal alignment. But there are other resemblances that cross the pairings. The second expanse from the top has a protrusion on its right side which, if flipped around, could fit inside the right-hand opening of the rightmost expanse, like a puzzle piece (see details). As we think about that opening, we become aware that the topmost expanse has a red hole in it that matches in shape the outline of the rightmost expanse. So the shapes, though organic and asymmetrical, are by no means arbitrarily hit upon.

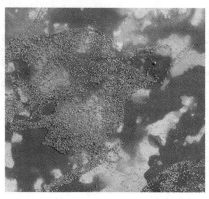

Fujimura, *Golden Countenance*, details: second expanse from the top, rightmost expanse.

All the expanses feather out in places into fine wisps of gold, which can be compared to the red beneath. It too bleeds out in wisps in the margins. Notice the marked similarities of shape between the gold and the red. Though none are identical—as shadows might be to their sources—they are close enough in form to invite our comparison. The red blotches are like distorted shadows of the gold, as if the gold's shadows had been refracted through some otherworldly fluid that thus transformed them. And speaking of shadows, the gold's actual three-dimensional surface casts its own this-worldly shadow on the surface of the image as well, to complicate and enhance the relation between red and gold by making the red sometimes seem closer to crimson.

Because the color of the gold is indebted to red, it seems all the more gold because of it. Red is one component used in mixing pigments to produce gold-colored paint. But Fujimura uses actual gold here, not gold-colored paint. Gold, unlike paint, reflects more light than it absorbs. So the red in the image actually reflects off of the surfaces of the gold dust, causing it to send yet more red out to our eyes, just as a candle set in front of a mirror brings twice as much light into the room.

While studying the red portions through the gold, we become

aware that they themselves do not seem to share a single plane of space. Indeed, the red splotches seem closest at the center of the image and extend deeply back and to the left but also bow around slightly to the right as well. The Nihonga technique Fujimura uses involves hand-ground materials which can be pulverized more or less coarsely to make them more or less completely saturate hand-made paper. So Fujimura can control the sense of depth in his images by allowing his inks to bleed out more or less completely. This suggestion of space, combined with the arrangement of the blotches of red and groups of gold dust, draws the viewer's eye down and then back up like a large checkmark across the image. Thanks to what seemed at first like an arbitrary organization of material, we are invited subconsciously to track the image over and over, never quite resting in the center but never drifting far from it.

Fujimura regularly uses programmatic titles for his works, which invite the viewer to bring certain associations. In this case the second word of the title is the most provocative, drawing up associations of the Aaronic blessing and the countenance of Jehovah. Like that countenance, the gold on the surface is brilliant and echoes itself in an image bearer to be found in the red.

A FLIGHT FROM MEANING: PETER JACKSON'S *FELLOWSHIP OF THE RING*, "FLIGHT TO THE FORD"

Without a contrasting example from our popular culture, readers may be left to assume that the kind of articulate visual design to be found in the images above is to be found in the same density in popular culture. In order to be fair, we have chosen as our contrasting example a highly regarded scene from Peter Jackson's *The Fellowship of the Ring*. The film is the first of a trilogy that is among the most cherished expressions of art in the lives of many Christians and non-Christians alike. We choose film, not still art, because popular culture does not normally use still images for artistic expression. Our example scene describes the flight of Arwen from the Ring-wraiths, with Frodo in her arms.

The first thing to notice about this scene is the rate at which cameras change. Excepting one eleven-second-long shot at the opening, the longest we are ever given to contemplate anything we see in this scene, before we are given a completely different view, is five seconds. On average, we are given two seconds. No one can get a good look at anything in two seconds. But two seconds is plenty of time to look at something for the sake merely of acknowledging its presence. A quick glimpse in a rearview mirror is all one ever needs. So we flash from one horse's face to another one's hooves, then back to Arwen, then to Frodo, then to an overall view, then back to horses' faces again, literally in the time it takes to read this sentence. Yes, this does announce the plot to us—it is a horse race—but it also forbids us to look at anything beyond the plot, since we are never given more than a few seconds to look.

The next thing to notice is that it wouldn't matter if we were given more than two seconds, because what little we do see in the scene is not very meaningful. Often it is a blur of tree branches or close-up shots of implausible horses' heads. Whatever we see clearly is gratuitously exaggerated. The wraiths' horses foam at the bit and open their mouths as if they planned on eating Arwen. Their bridles are irrational, being neither horse armor nor a simple snaffle bridle, but they make the horses fit expectations of Hollywood bad guys. Burglars are to wear balaclavas and wraiths' horses are, we suppose, to wear black face masks. They turn their heads from side to side and even back at the riders, as if being pulled up by the reins, though pulling up a horse in such a gallop would cause it to roll. But the reality of a horse chase is not exciting enough. It has to be enhanced.

A close-up of a wraith's hand opens above Frodo's head with all the menacing gesture of a children's pantomime. The frightening aspect of the wraiths has been conformed to the look of 1980s horror films. Tolkien himself describes wraiths as invisible and most fearful when unrobed.[1] Their black robes are necessary only to allow them to be seen by others. But postmoderns are not menaced by invisibility; they are comforted by it. The formlessness and void doesn't frighten them, but only trick-or-treat specters dressed in black, flapping rags, wearing reptilian armor. But none of this matters much because we are never invited to look at these wraiths or their horses.

As Arwen and the wraiths exit the forest and enter the clearing, we flash up to an aerial view to see that the wraiths have formed an inverted V around Arwen. This is to heighten the sense that she will soon be surrounded by her pursuers, though it is not clear why the rider in the rear cannot catch up to his colleagues and, therefore, to their prey. The imminence of doom must never wane. Any slack in the action may wake the viewers, like stopping in traffic may wake the baby in the car seat.

After this the course of the horse race is a little muddled due to faster flipping between cameras. We don't know how we have found ourselves suddenly back into woods, but we have. And this involves jumping over obstacles and some dressage. Wraiths appear first on this side and then the next, like bogies in a haunted house. Finally Arwen enters a wide, shallow stream, which the wraiths are unwilling to cross. This gives opportunity for Arwen to stop and challenge the wraiths to come into the stream. The camera surges forward when she says, in the intonation of melodrama, "If you want him, come and claim him." ("Claim," because it creates slant alliteration and therefore seems fancy, not because it makes sense.) She is neither sweating nor panting. Thanks to this close-up, we have another two whole seconds to look at the actress's beautiful face—made all the more attractive, according to popular fancy, by the mild cut on her right cheek.

Then, in a synchronized gesture, the wraiths draw their swords

---

[1] J. R. R. Tolkien, *Unfinished Tales* (New York: Ballantine, 1988), 358.

and wave them in the air. This is supposed to be frightening. But had the trance-inducing soundtrack not suspended the audience's natural affections, the gesture would seem preposterous because it is as choreographed as synchronized swimming. It mimics Hollywood battle scenes, not the manifest reality of battle—elven or human. Throughout, poor Frodo has been hanging his head and goggling as convincingly as a little boy who is trying to feign sick in order to skip school. In Tolkien's version, it is Frodo himself who is the rider. It is he who commands the wraiths to turn back, with an evocation of Elbereth and Lúthien the Fair.[2] Jackson has placed Arwen as the rider, we must assume, because the idea of a pretty heroine standing off against a pack of Ring-wraiths plays to the popular interest in women wielding swords.

Arwen's hair is now blown by a gentle, unbroken wind. This, along with the gentle panting that has suddenly come upon her, is meant, one supposes, to make her especially attractive. She then begins speaking Elvish, which takes on a strange digital echo so that we know that she is casting a charm. With lowered face, she looks penetratingly into the camera, but we don't know why. Does the charm have something to do with *me*? If it weren't for the incongruity of the moment, we would call it an alluring look.[3] Thanks to another two-second screen shot, we are alerted to the fact that the stream is swelling. Then, another glimpse tells us that a torrent is coming downstream. The wraiths are then washed up, and Arwen and Frodo are saved.

Whatever one can say about such a scene, one must say that it is calculated. The multiplicity of cameras, the elaborate system of special effects, and all the long hours of editing prove that the final shot is exactly what Jackson wanted from the scene. But what is it that he wanted? We learn almost nothing of horses, of the characters, or of even fear itself. We learn nothing about the landscape

---

[2] J. R. R. Tolkien, *The Fellowship of the Ring* (London: HarperCollins, 1997), 209.
[3] It seems remarkably similar to the look the actress presents in the release poster of her first big hit, *Stealing Beauty*, though there, she wears it and little else, leaving no doubt as to its meaning.

and little of the nature of the Ring-wraiths (who speak intelligibly at the ford in Tolkien's novel). We learn nothing except to be excited because a chase is going on. Much of the scene can be justified only because, by constant motion, it forces the viewer never to stop watching, just like flashing road signs attract attention. It causes us to forget that we are in a movie theater, that we have other things we could be doing with our two hours, that we have a last name.

Key to the success of ugly leisure is that it keeps those who participate in it in the dark about how little it is they get for their time invested. But we could read the corresponding passage in the book three times over in the time that it takes Jackson to convey his horse race and have a great deal more for our time. Consider one paragraph from Tolkien's original by comparison:

> Fear now filled all Frodo's mind. He thought no longer of his sword. No cry came from him. He shut his eyes and clung to the horse's mane. The wind whistled in his ears, and the bells upon the harness rang wild and shrill. A breath of deadly cold pierced him like a spear, as with a last spurt, like a flash of white fire, the elf-horse speeding as if on wings, passed right before the face of the foremost Rider.[4]

Notice how many of the senses are touched. We feel the horse hair (and do so with our own intellects, rather than having them commandeered from without). We hear the wind, here described to be as musical as a whistle. That combines with the sound of the bells in the horse's harness. We have the touch of deadly cold and then the heat of white fire. We see and feel more in this one paragraph than in the whole scene from the film, and yet it is film that is the *visual* medium. This is not to say that there might not be something worthwhile in the film, but that we spend badly our hours of leisure on such a thing when we could be enjoying innumerable better things, three of which have been described above.

---

[4] Tolkien, *Fellowship of the Ring*, 208.

✚ 5

LISTENING TO MUSIC

When the modern composer Edgard Varèse described music as "organized sound," he coined what has become perhaps the most widely accepted and least controversial definition of music. Nobody contradicts it because, obviously, all music does consist of sounds that have been organized. However, everybody can think of organized sounds that aren't called "music"—say, the dialing of a telephone—so the definition, like many uncontroversial things, does not satisfy. It says nothing of music's purposes (which are different from a telephone's). It does nothing to explain *why* humans organize sounds in musical ways.

Thinkers committed to a materialist framework, relying above all on evolutionary theory, have developed various answers to this question. Some say that music is merely a by-product of the evolutionary process that generated language. An organism must understand and delight in complex sounds if it is to use speech. Language, then, not music, is the relevant genetic adaptation propagated by evolutionary forces, with music being an accidental result of that adaptation.[1] Another explanation uses Darwin's idea of sexual selection to uncover music's real function: to maximize men's reproductive success.[2] When a woman is attracted to someone so clever that he can make music, her offspring are more likely to survive, both because they may be nurtured by a clever father and because they will carry his clever genes. This accounts

---

[1] A famous formulation of this argument can be read in Steven Pinker's *How the Mind Works* (New York: Norton, 1997).
[2] See, e.g., Geoffrey F. Miller, *The Mating Mind* (New York: Anchor, 2001).

for how a rock star can have success with the ladies even if he's not handsome.

By contrast, ordinary people tend to explain the power of music (very sensibly, we think) not according to a biological function but according to a social function: we care about music because of what it communicates to us. And what does it communicate? Here, most people struggle a bit. They know it causes them to feel emotional, but they don't understand how; after all, music seems so abstract compared to other semantic systems like language and pictures. So they conclude that what music communicates is emotion itself. It seems plausible enough. But it's rather like saying, by analogy, that what sunsets communicate is emotion, which doesn't seem so plausible. One would have to be heartless not to emote in response to a sunset, certainly, but what it communicates is far greater than human emotion (Ps. 19:1). Similarly, we don't go to a concert to learn how sad or happy the musician (or anybody else) is. We go to hear something more universal and permanent. This is not to belittle the expression of emotion in human interaction. When someone says, "Hooray!" or, "That hurt," healthy souls respond sympathetically; but it's incomparably more moving to learn what lies behind the "Hooray." Similarly, at a concert we study things worthy of emotion, and that leaves us more emotionally alive than a mere expression of emotion ever could.

The Christian intellectual tradition looks to the Bible for an explanation of music's role in human life. The very first chapter of Genesis tells us that God charged the human race to rule the earthly order for his glory. It's what we were made to do. For example, when engineers make a bridge to afford easy and safe passage over a river, when motorists benefit from that bridge, and when bridge fanciers take pleasure in it, they glorify the Creator of tension, of compression, and all other forces involved, as well as the God who cares about the productivity and safety of his human creatures. Similarly, when musicians arrange tones and rhythms to reveal their interrelatedness, their potential for harmony, and their potential as materials for design, they glorify a Creator so wise that he could endow sounds with such properties, and so good that he placed his human creatures in a world that contains these sounds.

In this way, music communicates the character and providential oversight of God and, therefore, naturally elicits emotions from souls made to worship him. We emote in response to moral reality, which is what music is. It communicates goodness and truth. Music presents us, directly, with propositions about sound and time (a certain pattern of notes can reach a certain end via a certain design) and, indirectly, with propositions about the Lord of sound and time (the pattern has this capacity because of his wisdom, power, and goodness). Ugly music is ugly because it lies. It suppresses, advertently or inadvertently, the truth and goodness of creation and providence. Sad music pleases us by speaking truthfully (in tones and rhythms) about the effect of the fall and the law's curse on creation (as when certain dissonances or a formal dilemma issue with compelling logic from a song's "premises"). Happy music moves us the way it does by speaking truthfully about grace and hope in a new creation.

Only music's potential for communicating the good and the true explains why we find such succor in it. There our sin-tossed souls encounter proof that meaning informs some of the most basic things in reality. In George MacDonald's *At the Back of the North Wind*, Diamond asks North Wind how she can bear to sink a passenger ship in her storm:

> I will tell you how I am able to bear it, Diamond: I am always hearing, through every noise, through all the noise I am making myself even, the sound of a far-off song. I do not exactly know where it is, or what it means; and I don't hear much of it, only the odour of its music, as it were, flitting across the great billows of the ocean outside this air in which I make such a storm; but

what I do hear, is quite enough to make me able to bear the cry
from the drowning ship. So it would you if you could hear it.[3]

North Wind speaks of something we already know, even if we are
rarely conscious of it. She speaks of the song of divine creation
and providence, which is there for all to contemplate (if only we
hadn't become futile in our thinking) and of which human songs
are echoes, various in fidelity.

The hearing of these echoes brings pleasure to people of
all ages and cultures, whether they be children chanting on the
playground, dancers following their steps and floor patterns, or a
scholar ruminating over a fugue. The only problem is that without
the grace of Christ, the child, the dancer, and the scholar cannot
be honest with themselves about what it is they are enjoying, and,
in the end, their rebellion will spoil all their pleasure.

Christians, however, can expect their appetite for God's glory
to increase for eternity. Those who would grow in their enjoyment
of it musically can do so by growing in their ability to hear the
sounds of music and the way they are organized. Consider a culinary analogy. A little child enjoys the way candy bursts with sweet-
ness in his mouth. An adult enjoys the way sweet amino acids and
sugars in Japanese tea interact with bitter caffeine and astringent
catechin to produce layers and sequences of flavors. In one sense,
the child may seem more delighted than the dignified practitioner
of a tea ceremony; jumping up and down in front of the gumball
machine, the child's sheer physical excitement is evident. But, considered objectively, in terms of what is enjoyed, the adult has more
potential for joy because he has more to enjoy. So, too, with music.

Although the mental activity of enjoying music is complex, or
so psychologists and neurologists tell us, for the purposes of this
chapter it can be broken down into just three parts: perception,
memory, and contemplation. A person enjoying music must, first,

<hr>
[3] George MacDonald, *At the Back of the North Wind* (New York: Knopf, 2001), chap. 7, "The
Cathedral."

hear what's happening in the music. Then he must *remember* what happened earlier so that, third, he can *reflect* on why the music has unfolded like this. People who haven't developed these faculties can only enjoy music in rudimentary ways: the impulse of the dance and the timbres of the moment. As they musically mature, they begin to enjoy melody, harmony, and, eventually, the development of musical ideas over spans of time. Those who relish music want to *hear* the details, which is why they value live performances and high-fidelity recordings on well-engineered playback equipment. They don't want to miss an internal voice, for example, or a subtle shift in color. Those who relish music *remember* the details and *reflect* on how they relate to one another, which is why they like to give music their full attention and why they prefer to listen in settings free from distraction.

A SHORT EXAMPLE

We ask the reader to find a good, legal recording of Antonio Vivaldi's Violin Concerto in E Major, Opus 8, Number 1, RV 269, also called *Spring* (*La Primavera*) from *The Four Seasons* (*Le quattro stagioni*). You will notice this work consists of three portions, called "movements," usually recorded on separate tracks.

Learning something about the stylistic era and genre of a musical work can give one a sense of what to listen for, but it's not strictly necessary. Far more critical to the success of one's listening is simply a willingness to *listen carefully*, whether or not one knows what a "concerto" is. That said, basic historical background is usually provided in CD booklets or can be found in readily available reference works such as Wikipedia articles. Or one might read the music appreciation and music history texts recommended at the end of this book. For the work before us, it's helpful to know that Vivaldi published an Italian sonnet (written by himself?) to declare what is depicted in the music. We will be discussing the first movement only, which treats lines 1–8 of this sonnet:

Giunt'è la Primavera e festosetti	Spring has arrived, and festively
La salutan gl'augei con lieto canto,	the birds greet her [Spring] with a happy song;
E i fonti allo spirar de' zeffiretti	and streams, under the breath of gentle breezes,
Con dolce mormorio scorrono intanto:	flow with a sweet murmur.
Vengon' coprendo l'aer di nero amanto	The air is covered by a black cloak; thunder and
E lampi, e tuoni ad annuntiarla eletti	lightning are chosen to announce Spring's arrival;
Indi tacendo questi, gl'augelletti	when they fall silent, the little birds take up again
Tornan' di nuovo al lor canoro incanto:	their melodious song.

Please listen to the first movement before reading any further.

The opening melody depicting the coming of spring is merry and dance-like with even a hint of foot stamping (hear the repeated notes of the bass line). If we label each phrase with a letter, we can describe the form of this melody as AABB, with each phrase lasting about seven seconds and then softly repeating itself. If you feel a sense of happy expectancy, it may come from the way the A-phrase leaps up twice to a high note and then holds it. In the more insistent B-phrase, that same high, long note appears not twice but three times.

Then come the birds, back from their southern migration. Three violin soloists imitate the clamor of various songbirds, simultaneously calling in carefree disregard of one another. After that comes something familiar. (Did you try to identify it when listening on your own?) It's the B-phrase of the opening melody, played just once. Note the time on your recording when it begins (around 0:58 in the fastest performances, and 1:09 in the slowest performances) and compare it to the B-phrase at the beginning of the movement (around 0:14), and you will detect no change at all. The birds do not effect, but merely adorn, the metamorphosis of spring.

Then comes another sound we all associate with spring: running water. The poem refers to Zephyr, the mild west wind that, in the Mediterranean world, brings the thaw. The orchestra performs a rippling figure, irregularly repeated to suggest currents of moving water. When the B-phrase returns next, once again take note of the time on your recording (1:25 in the fastest performances, and 1:46 in the slowest) and compare it, back to back, with its first appearance (0:14). Everything on the surface of the tune—its rhythms and outline—remains the same, and yet it sounds strangely different. Unless you have studied music, you may find it impossible to describe just what this difference is; but if you sing along with the recording in these places, you'll notice that the orchestra is now playing lower pitches. It is playing in a different key. (Baroque concertos often do this. An arrival in a new key is marked by having the orchestra play something familiar in that key, to measure for us the distance we have come.) While the birds of spring do not really change anything, the warmer air certainly does.

Then comes a spring storm. The orchestra rumbles, a virtuosic violin soloist crackles. When the B-phrase comes around again, not only is it in yet a third key, but it has switched from *major mode* to *minor mode*. This means some of the intervals of the melody and harmony have been altered to create a darker and less stable sound. Spring is not always happy.

When the storm subsides, we hear something else that sounds familiar. It's the birds, peeking out from their hiding places. If they sound more cautious than before, it's because they have learned from experience!

At some point, the music has to bring us back to the home key. Anticipating this, the music we hear after the reprise of birdsong is the most expectant of the whole movement. It resolves finally in a twofold statement of the B-phrase (loud, then soft) at the very end of the movement and in the home key, creating a huge sense of return and closure.

The imagery of the poem is charming. And in an exercise like that just completed, it aids inexperienced listeners in keeping track of musical events. But the piece would still be quite enjoyable even if we knew nothing about the poem. Without it, we would hear an abstract adventure, "there and back again" (to quote Tolkien), unfolding in a series of contrasting and related passages coordinated in various kinds of departures and returns. Actually, most Western music works this way. A rock song, for example, "departs" through changes of verse and bridge, and "returns" with a chorus. When familiar material returns, we don't hear it the same as we did before, having learned what happens in the intervening passages.

Let's listen next to a piece that has no extramusical references whatsoever and try our hand at hearing this kind of narrative-without-words.

A LONGER EXAMPLE

Find a recording of the first movement of Franz Schubert's Symphony No. 8 in B Minor, "Unfinished," and listen to it before proceeding. (If you find it a tad bewildering the first time through, that's okay. Listen to it more than once. You will assuredly hear more and more every time. Unfortunately, many older recordings disregard Schubert's clear instruction that the first three or so minutes of the movement—which musicians call the "exposition"—be repeated. We recommend the celebrated recording conducted by Carlos Kleiber, but if you cannot find that, at least find one that takes the repeat. An easy way to tell this is by the length of the first movement. If it's under thirteen minutes, the repeat has been skipped. If it's over thirteen minutes, Schubert's instruction has been followed.)

What did you think of the opening? Very softly, without any accompaniment, the lowest instruments climb two steps, fall back down, and then keep descending until they're considerably lower than where they began. The phrase ends not like a statement but like a question—perhaps an ominous one. We print the melody here in musical notation to help readers think about the contour.

First Melody

The strangest thing about the melody is that this one phrase is all we get of it. For perspective, recall the opening of the *Spring Concerto* with its two phrases, both repeated, and bear in mind that Vivaldi's movement is only one-fourth as long as Schubert's. How can such a long story begin with something so fleeting? The word *laconic* comes to mind.

There is a stirring high above the abyss, as violins begin to play a rustling figure that could almost be taken for a second melody, except that it turns out to be accompaniment to something even more interesting: the real second melody shared by an oboe and a clarinet.

Second Melody

To describe the expressive effect of this melody, it's helpful to know something about *mode*: the ordering of whole steps and half steps in music. Western music generally has two modes: major and minor. Major mode tends to sound brighter and more stable than does minor mode. (Recall the effect of the storm in Vivaldi's *Spring Concerto*; or compare "Hark! the herald angels sing," which is in major, with "When Johnny comes marching home again, hurrah, hurrah," which is in minor.) The oboe and clarinet melody is restless, perhaps in reaction to the preceding shadows. It tries to move beyond a plaintive, minor mode beginning, to close in a major key (the last note printed in our extract) but is straightaway, almost simultaneously, shoved back to its original key and mode—and that of the ominous first melody—by the first loud sound of the symphony. The melody grows through two subsequent phrases, each of which seeks to close in that same major key, only to be checked by ever more violent interruptions. The last of these will brook no opposition.

Everything freezes as horns and bassoons sustain a single note for a long time: a counterpart to the ominous first melody's last note. It pivots to a major key (not, however, the key sought by the second melody), and we hear a third melody. This one sings:

Third Melody

As the second melody began by falling from *sol* to *do* (from F#, the fifth note of a B-minor scale, to B, the first note of the scale), the third melody begins by falling from *do* to *sol* (from G, the first note of a G-major scale, to D, the fifth note of the scale). The gesture has been switched around. The state of mind has, too, from restless to calm—to a calm that seems naive, even, given what has come before. As you study the printed quotation of the third melody, notice that its first two notes return at the end of the phrase, and that the first three notes of the second measure return at the beginning of the third measure, so the melody sounds like a happy little palindrome (think "radar" or "kayak"). Even sweeter phrases follow. Then, after forty seconds or so the melody unexpectedly breaks off, mid-phrase, as if spooked. There is an awful silence. Violent chords lead to a dialog between low strings and high strings obsessing over the third measure of the third melody.

Look again at that third measure (in the extract above, the notes between the second and the third vertical line). It climbs two steps, *like the beginning of the first melody*, falls, and climbs again by two steps. What upsets the third melody is its relationship to the first melody—the foreboding one. In fact, the third melody broke off (before the violent chords, as described in the previous paragraph) just as it was climbing two steps.

Third Melody, "Spooked"

Eventually, the first three (or three and a half) minutes of the movement close with a variant of the third melody, soothed to something like its original calm. As mentioned earlier, authentic performances repeat everything heard up to this point, giving you a second chance to learn these ideas and how they relate to one another, before continuing.

Anybody who enjoys stories knows what comes next. Thus far, we have been learning the main musical ideas and how they relate to one another; now those ideas and relations should evolve in a series of increasingly interesting events, which English teachers would call the "rising action" plus "climax," but which musicians call the "development." As this section begins, curious listeners are full of questions, hopes, and fears. Will the second melody achieve some kind of stability in the major mode? Or will it give up? Can we expect more violent interruptions in the development section? What would that sound like? Alternatively, can the third melody do anything to consolidate the relative peace with which the exposition closed? It comes as something of a shock, then, when the listener realizes that all such questions were off the mark. Neither the second nor the third melody, it turns out, plays an overt role in the development section.

Performances of this section of the movement range in length from three to three and three-quarters minutes, and, in all that time, all we hear is development of the first melody—the very melody that was so tight-lipped in the exposition. We have noted the constraining influence it exerted on the other melodies from the beginning. As initially surprising as it is for us now to hear the laconic melody reappear in such long-winded grandeur, it begins to make sense. This is a story about the potential for hidden, underlying causes to have extensive consequences.

The last major section in the first movement of a symphony is called the "recapitulation." (English teachers would call it the "falling action" plus "dénouement.") It normally begins with a passage that sounds exactly like the beginning of the exposition, then works its way through all the materials of the exposition, in the same order, transforming them in ways to suggest resolution or some other meaningful outcome. In this symphony, however, that moment-which-is-supposed-to-sound-like-the-beginning-of-the-exposition never arrives. After such a development section, it would be anticlimactic (and redundant) for the recapitulation to begin with the first melody in its original form. Instead, it starts right off with the rustling violin accompaniment to the second melody. In following passages, the second melody and then the third melody undergo several subtle transformations, which we interpret in light of what has happened. Finally, in the end, no one is surprised to hear the first melody have the last word, for it has proved to be the real subject of the movement.

A COUNTEREXAMPLE

If you are still reading at this point, having listened carefully to the Vivaldi and the Schubert, you have heard something of what makes careful listening rewarding, if a bit strenuous. We would like to end the book by suggesting an experiment. If you haven't done so already, try listening with this same care to your favorite music. Try to *hear* everything in it, to *recall* it so as to compare one passage with another, and to *reflect* on what makes it meaningful. The Christian doctrine of general revelation teaches us that the purpose of things in this world is to speak, and that we were made to listen, so we should not be surprised if all the best pleasures come from paying attention. Try it. You may find that you enjoy that song more than ever before. Or you may find that your ideas of what it means to enjoy music are expanding.

What follows is one instance of such a trial. In May 2012 we surveyed several classes to identify a song that is highly esteemed by the largest possible number of our students. The clear winner was Mumford & Sons' "The Cave," for which we now ask you to find a recording and, if possible, a copy of the lyrics. Please listen to it prior to reading the following.

Let's begin with the words. For many listeners, the title brings to mind Plato's famous allegory of ignorance and education from book 7 of *The Republic*. The first three-line verse seems to confirm this when, as in Plato, somebody walks away into the sunlight, leaving something behind. The verse's opening reference to a valley is disconcerting, however. Is the word "valley" substituted for "cave" to emphasize some property of the cave that it shares with valleys? The connection to Plato's cave weakens when we learn the thing left behind is not ignorance but fears and faults. The only clear reference to a cave does not occur until the fifth verse, where the allusion is unquestionably to a much less famous book: chapter 5 of G. K. Chesterton's *St. Francis of Assisi*. Whereas Plato's cave is the setting of something bad (imprisonment and error), Chesterton's is a setting of something good (Francis's transformation into a saint). We are left with a number of questions about the basic meaning of the title image, which are never answered.

The other images prove just as inscrutable, disconnected, and undeveloped. The "you" who is walking away from his fears and faults is, it turns out, a cannibal disappointed by a harvest. Presumably we're not meant to take this literally, but it's not evident how the metaphors are supposed to work. The speaker then assures the cannibal that the speaker (that is, "I") can identify with his "defeat," but we have no idea in what way and why defeat was accomplished. In the chorus we learn that the cannibal has a noose around his or her neck, and that he or she is going to choke "on" it, as if he or she were eating the rope—that is, the rope that we're told is "around" his or her neck. This is the stuff of madness or erratic nightmares, not articulate speech. It would be laborious for us to continue line by line in this way, but there's no avoiding the fact that were a person to speak to us in this way, we would not say that he was being poetic or even reciting a poem; we would say he was babbling.

Not that the poem is devoid of poetic elements. The first three verses and chorus are in an iambic meter (following the rhythmic pattern da-DUM da-DUM da-DUM da-DUM da-DUM). This is largely abandoned, however, in verses 4 and 5 and the pre-chorus. It's unclear how a shift from metrical regularity to the rhythms of prose is supposed to underscore the message of a song about changing one's ways and growing in wisdom.

There are also occasional rhymes and assonant line endings. But these irregular rhymes themselves only add to the meaninglessness of the text. In the third verse we are to rhyme "time" with "mine" and "mind," although these aren't real rhymes. But thanks to all this effort to create rhyme, we end up with all sorts of ambiguity. We have no sense for what things had been filling the speaker's time before he found these other things to fill it with. We have no idea what could possibly be "yours" and what "mine." (Is this the same "I" who promised not to let "you" choke?) And we discover that somehow "you" is going to let "I" at the truth that will refresh his broken mind, even though broken things need to be mended, not refreshed.

Verse 4 begins with an image that is actually clear, even vivid, if of uncertain relevance to the rest of the song. The speaker, alluding to Homer's *Odyssey*, wants both the protection Odysseus obtained from the sirens' song by being tied to the mast of his ship and the protection his men obtained by having their ears stopped up with beeswax.

But that's as good as the poem gets. Neither we nor anyone else can have any idea what the song means. Oh, we get that its topic has something to do with the speaker's resolve to stay the course and to grow, even as someone else does something else. But who the speaker is, who the someone else is, what the course is, and what the growth is, is anybody's guess. The poem says nothing clear about anything. For indirect confirmation of this, read what people have to say about "The Cave" on Internet lyrics forums. For some it's about overcoming addiction. For others it's about reaching enlightenment or trying to get out from a narrow-minded community, or breaking up and finding life after a relationship. There's nothing close to a consensus about what the song means. Nor can there be, because the song is meaningless. Perhaps that's why it's appealing. Meaningless things are appealing, because they allow us to talk to ourselves in front of them without distracting us with their own meaning. Their vagueness offers us a framework for our own ideas without imposing ideas of their own (see chapter 3).

Listening to the music, we find that it, too, is short on meaning. The introductory riff consists of a guitar gesture that repeats, repeats again, and then cadences (or closes). The same music reappears in the first instrumental interlude and, assigned to the singer, in the verses. Since there are five verses, this means we hear the same gesture *twenty-one* times (3×7), without a trace of development. The only other music in the song is that of the chorus (the chorus and the pre-chorus being musically the same).

This chorus is the saving grace of the song because, while it in no way extends or develops the fragmentary melody of the verse, it does develop within itself. The high, held note on "I" returns a step higher in the second half of the chorus, at "I'll." Moreover—and this is actually pretty lucid—the held note on "I" is a high *sol* (fifth note of the scale), and the held note on "I'll" is a high *la* (sixth note of the scale). One octave lower and in reverse order, these were the two most important notes in the verse: "It's empty in the VAL-ley of your HEART." (Or listen for the two notes that ring out in the introductory guitar riff.) So although it is true that the chorus relates in no melodic way to the verse, there is a structural connection. In a song about finding strength and changing one's ways, the two most important notes of the verse's repeated gesture return in the chorus at a higher level of perception—in a higher octave, longer in duration, and in ascending order. Then, at the end of the song, the corresponding notes in the third chorus ("I" and "I'll") are sung higher yet, on high *do* (the first note of the scale).

Still, listening carefully to "The Cave" brings comparatively scant rewards. This suggests that those who like it are doing something other than listening carefully when they are liking it. To paraphrase the first page of *An Experiment in Criticism,* if we say that A likes (or has a taste for) Mumford & Sons and that B likes (or has a taste for) Schubert, this sounds as if *likes* has the same meaning when applied to both; as if there were a single activity, though the objects to which it is directed are different. But observation convinces us that this is untrue.

COMPARING GREAT MUSIC AND POPULAR MUSIC

What is the difference?

It's not that great music is more complex than popular music. Many popular songs involve complex rhythm (especially syncopation). The texture is rich in places (note the trumpet countermelody at the very end of "The Cave"). Some popular songs employ key changes and chromatic harmony. Some popular musicians put a lot of thought into the sound, or timbre, of their music. Furthermore, some great music is simple. An art song by Schubert, say, or a theme and variations by Mozart can go some time without any of these complexities.

Nor is it that classical music is more intellectual than popular music. All the most important things in Schubert's Symphony No. 8 can be appreciated by a thoughtful child.

Nor is it that one is more emotional than the other.

Nor is it that popular music altogether lacks beauty. Witness the twist on Homer's siren story or the melodic development of the chorus.

The difference is that in popular music those few beautiful thoughts do not work together to mean much. The main gesture in the verses of "The Cave" cannot be called anything more than a "gesture" because there's nothing more articulate that can be said about it. It does not initiate a progression of thought but merely repeats over and over again. Then when something different finally happens at the beginning of the chorus, it's somewhat more interesting than the verse, but that's not saying much. The pleasure to be had from contemplating the relation between the two—between the only two musical ideas in the song—is meager. Putting the lyrics and the music together, we gather that the song is about changing one's ways. But what those changes and ways are remains vague.

So why would anyone, if they have a spare hour, listen to Mumford & Sons instead of Schubert? In our many conversations with people who like popular music, there are five elements of the music that consistently appear to attract them: familiarity, loudness, accumulation (via repetition, added layers of texture, or increasing loudness), an irresistible dance impulse, and what is often described as a "cool" sound. All of these have little to do with meaning. They are sensations. We can only conclude that part of the attraction of such a song—and, by extension, of popular culture—is that it says almost nothing. It's a way of filling one's free time with sensation without meaning. When we ask rock connoisseurs about what they like, they speak additionally of innovation and virtuosity: so-and-so does new and technically amazing things with his guitar. But the reader can see how that's an entirely different aesthetic world from Schubert's.[4]

His Eighth Symphony, without the advantage of words, presents a musical narrative that thoroughly and coherently explores the possibilities of its materials. In so doing, it reveals the glory of the one who created sound and time and who sovereignly directs things to their appointed end.

So our overview of Christian thought on aesthetics and the enjoyment of art and music ends with a very personal question: Do you delight in God's gifts? In particular, are you using your discretionary time to savor as much of God's goodness as you can, as it has been revealed generally and specially? Do your choices of leisure activities leave your soul refreshed and more ready for the next day's labors of service and worship?

Do not stop with Schubert. For we know that the difference in meaningfulness between a Schubert symphony and the things to be contemplated in heaven is far greater—incomparably so—than the difference in meaningfulness between a Mumford & Sons song and a Schubert symphony. One of the most thrilling things about the Christian view of beauty is the assurance it gives of the possibility of growth. All who are united to Christ can, with unveiled faces, behold the glory of the Lord—and be transformed. And though we have eternity before us in which to grow in our appetite for beholding God's glory, there's no reason we can't start the process now.

---

[4] What people enjoy at the Olympic Games is different from what they enjoy in a concert hall, else we could easily devise more physically challenging performances by having the musicians stand on their heads.

TIMELINE

TIMELINE OF WORKS DISCUSSED

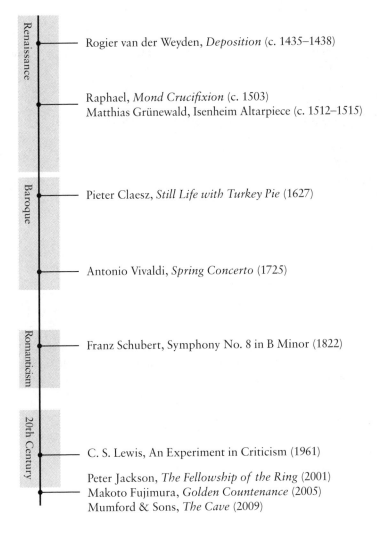

Renaissance

Rogier van der Weyden, *Deposition* (c. 1435–1438)

Raphael, *Mond Crucifixion* (c. 1503)
Matthias Grünewald, Isenheim Altarpiece (c. 1512–1515)

Baroque

Pieter Claesz, *Still Life with Turkey Pie* (1627)

Antonio Vivaldi, *Spring Concerto* (1725)

Romanticism

Franz Schubert, Symphony No. 8 in B Minor (1822)

20th Century

C. S. Lewis, An Experiment in Criticism (1961)

Peter Jackson, *The Fellowship of the Ring* (2001)
Makoto Fujimura, *Golden Countenance* (2005)
Mumford & Sons, *The Cave* (2009)

QUESTIONS FOR REFLECTION

1) Why am I not always a good judge of what, ultimately, will give me the most pleasure?

2) Why is general revelation necessary to our understanding of Scripture?

3) What is the difference between godly recreation and idleness?

4) Can I learn from a work of art or music that is partly true and partly false?

5) Questions for the gallery: To what is this work of art drawing my attention and how did it draw it there?

6) Questions for the concert: What are the main musical themes of this piece? Do they return? Are they the same upon returning? Or have they changed? Why?

GLOSSARY

Aesthetic relativism. The belief that an object is beautiful because someone believes that it is so. Aesthetic relativism supplies the expression "Beauty is in the eye of the beholder."

Aesthetics. A branch of philosophy dealing with formal value. As metaphysics and epistemology study truth and ethics studies goodness, so aesthetics studies beauty.

Baroque. Styles of European art and music from 1600–1750.

Chord. A combination of simultaneous notes.

Composition. In art, the arrangement of the materials of the work into a design. In music, a piece of music that is planned out (and, in some traditions, written out) before first performance.

Concerto. An orchestral work characterized by an unfolding relationship between a soloist (or group of soloists) and the orchestra. Usually in three movements.

Flanders. The portions of Belgium, France, and Holland that were once joined into a free Duchy of particularly rich artistic and musical output from the fifteenth through the eighteenth centuries.

Form. The shape in which something exists or the appearance by which it is known.

General revelation. "God's self-disclosure in a general way to all people at all times and all places. God reveals himself through nature, history, human experience, and human conscience."[1] It must be supplemented by the Bible, God's special revelation, by which he makes known his saving grace to sinners.

Harmony. That part of musical art dealing with the formation of chords and how they relate to one another. A melody is said to be "harmonized" when it is supported by chords.

Key. The sense we have that notes mean what they mean because of how they relate to one another in a hierarchical, harmonic system around a central pitch of reference. That referential pitch gives the key its name.

Mode. The ordering of whole steps and half steps in music. In minor mode, the third scale-degree and sometimes the sixth and seventh scale-degrees are a half step lower than in major mode, significantly affecting its structure and expressive effect.

Movement. A semi-independent part of an extended musical composition. A movement is to the composition as a whole as a chapter is to a book.

Nihonga. A style of painting that uses traditional Japanese materials and techniques.

Northern Renaissance. The seeming increase of artistic, musical, and (though less so) scholarly output in countries north of the Alps during the fifteenth and sixteenth centuries. Thought of as analogous to the Renaissance in Italy at the same time, which is usually described as *the* Renaissance by contrast.

Object. In philosophy, particularly in discussions of aesthetics, the thing being observed.

---

[1] David S. Dockery and Timothy George, *The Great Tradition of Christian Thinking: A Student's Guide* (Wheaton, IL: Crossway, 2012), 105.

Orientation. In art, when a work is not square shaped, a work's position in relation to the horizon line. Modern usage applies the term *portrait* to describe works whose long sides are perpendicular to the actual horizon, and *landscape* for works whose long sides are parallel to the horizon.

Subject. In philosophy, particularly in discussions of aesthetics, the mind doing the observing. Not to be confused with "subject matter," which in art refers to the objects portrayed.

Symphony. A composition for orchestra, usually in four movements, with the first movement typically having an exposition, development, and recapitulation.

Timbre. Tone color. Used, for example, to describe the difference in sound between a violin and a trumpet.

Vantage point. In art, the position in which the viewer is placed by the artist relative to whatever is being viewed. A high vantage point will look down on it, whereas a low one will look up at it.

RESOURCES FOR FURTHER STUDY

Authors' note: The principal resources for studying art and music are great works of art and music themselves.

AESTHETICS (ALL WRITTEN FROM A CHRISTIAN PERSPECTIVE, EXCEPT THE SCRUTON)

Balthasar, Hans Urs von. *The Glory of the Lord: A Theological Aesthetics.* Vol. 1, *Seeing the Form.* San Francisco: Ignatius, 1982.

Edwards, Jonathan. *A Dissertation Concerning the Nature of True Virtue*, chap. 3. In *The Works of Jonathan Edwards.* Vol. 1. Edinburgh: Banner of Truth, 1974.

———. *A Treatise Concerning Religious Affections*, part 3, sec. 4. In *The Works of Jonathan Edwards.* Vol. 1. Edinburgh: Banner of Truth, 1974.

Elmers, Elizabeth. *Beauty Unframed.* Mountain Home, AR: BorderStone, 2011.

Lewis, C. S. *An Experiment in Criticism.* Cambridge, UK: Cambridge University Press, 1961.

Myers, Kenneth A. *All God's Children and Blue Suede Shoes: Christians and Popular Culture.* Wheaton, IL: Crossway, 1989.

Ryken, Leland. *Culture in Christian Perspective: A Door to Understanding and Enjoying the Arts.* Portland, OR: Multnomah, 1986. Reprinted as *The Liberated Imagination: Thinking Christianly about the Arts.* Reprinted Eugene, OR: Wipf & Stock, 2005.

Ryken, Philip Graham. *Art for God's Sake.* Phillipsburg, NJ: P&R, 2006.

Scruton, Roger. *The Aesthetics of Music.* Oxford, UK: Oxford University Press, 1999.

Thomas Aquinas. *Summa Theologiae.* Prima pars, question 5, article 4; prima pars, question 39, article 8; prima secundæ partis, question 27, article 1; secunda secundæ partis, question 145, article 2.

Veith, Gene Edward, Jr. *State of the Arts: From Bezalel to Mapplethorpe.* Wheaton, IL: Crossway, 1991.

ART (NOT WRITTEN FROM AN EXPLICITLY CHRISTIAN PERSPECTIVE)

Stokstad, Marilyn. *Art History.* Any edition from the first (New York: H. N. Abrams, 1995) to the current, fifth edition (Boston: Pearson, 2013).

Taylor, Joshua C. *Learning to Look: A Handbook for the Visual Arts.* 2nd ed. Chicago: University of Chicago Press, 1981.

MUSIC (NOT WRITTEN FROM AN EXPLICITLY CHRISTIAN PERSPECTIVE)

Classics Today: Your Guide to Classical Music Online. Edited by David Vernier and David Hurwitz. http://www.classicstoday.com/.

Grout, Donald Jay. *A History of Western Music.* Any edition from the first (New York: Norton, 1960) to the current, ninth edition (New York: Norton, 2014).

Hurwitz, David. *Exploring Haydn: A Listener's Guide to Music's Boldest Innovator.* Pompton Plains, NJ: Amadeus, 2005.

Kamien, Roger. *Music: An Appreciation.* Any edition from the first (New York: McGraw-Hill, 1976) to the current, eleventh edition (Dubuque, IA: McGraw-Hill Education, 2014).

GENERAL INDEX

Page numbers in italics refer to figures.

SCRIPTURE INDEX

✚ CHECK OUT THE OTHER BOOKS IN THE
**RECLAIMING THE CHRISTIAN
INTELLECTUAL TRADITION SERIES**

For more information, visit crossway.org.